Inquiries should be addressed to:
Outside the Lines Publishing
PO Box 1094
Dryden, ON P8N 3E3
or
KLaurenPaige@gmail.com

ISBN: 978-0-9950777-0-6

Book & Jacket Design:
K'Lauren Paige

Look for my work at Amazon.com. Check us out on Facebook & www.klaurenpaige.com too !

K'Lauren is a wife and busy mum of three, with a penchant for whimsical art. Through life's hills and valleys, K'Lauren is no stranger to stress and copes by living simply and being silly. From her home in Northwestern Ontario, Canada, K'Lauren draws peace from each piece, letting the exhilaration and exhaustion of daily life pour out onto paper. Doodling is her chill time... maybe colouring is yours ?

Acknowledgements

MY BETTER HALF- A huge thank you to my biggest supporter and dearest friend, my husband, photographer, co-parent & technical advisor. You always said, "I can", when I thought I couldn't ...you're my world hon.

MY KIDS - From blue hair, Adventures of Oscar and Otto to itty bitty clay creations, my kids' creativity & curiosity remind me of the importance of taking time to play, to think outside the box and that there is always a point to doing something pointless.

ANNIE - For all your support & wonderful suggestions, for keeping my pen rolling and keeping me accountable. You paint in possibilities and have the insight of a sage. I'm grateful for your guidance.

ARTSY TALENT - The painters, musicians, photographers, sculptors & authors among my friends in social media land... your unique styles are brilliant and always an inspiration.

PALS - Near and far, you've been nothing but kind as I've worked toward this goal, and have taught me that our world has all the vibrancy of the rainbow.

KELLY & THE 12'ers - For all the laughs, as we lost our minds, found our happy place and devoured the crayons, among other things... I still say the purple one is graple flavoured and you bet your behind I ate it! (snort)

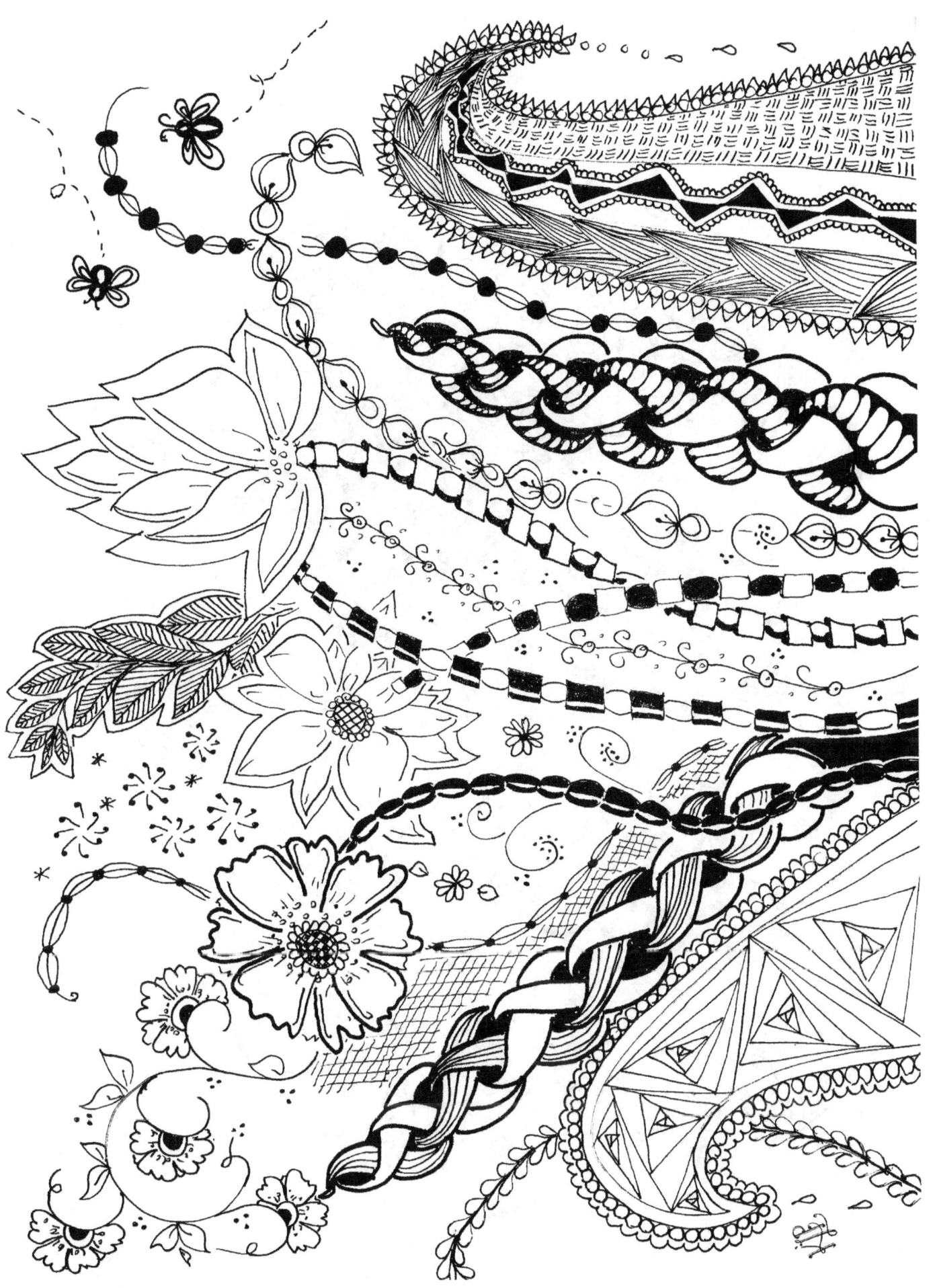

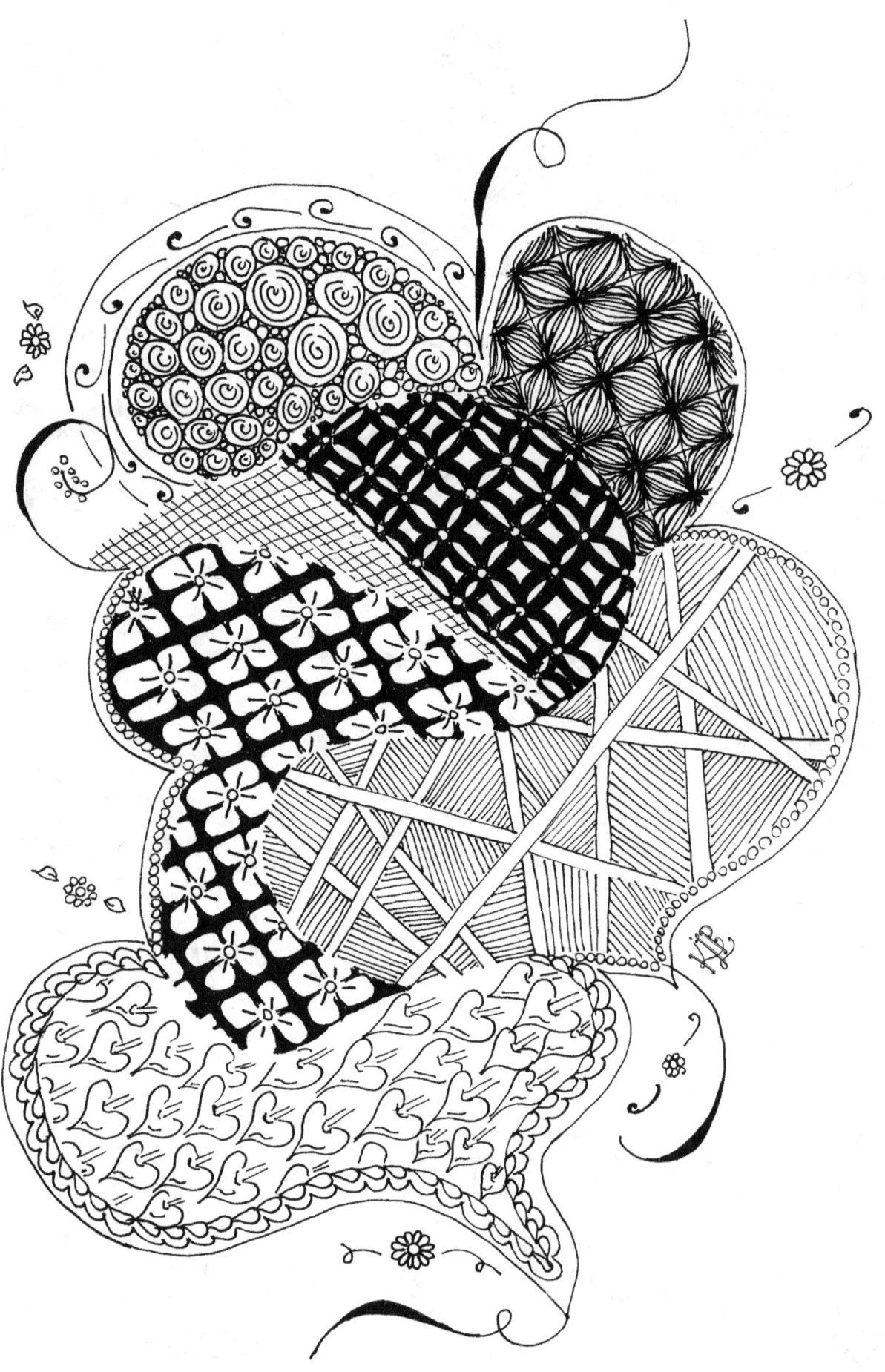

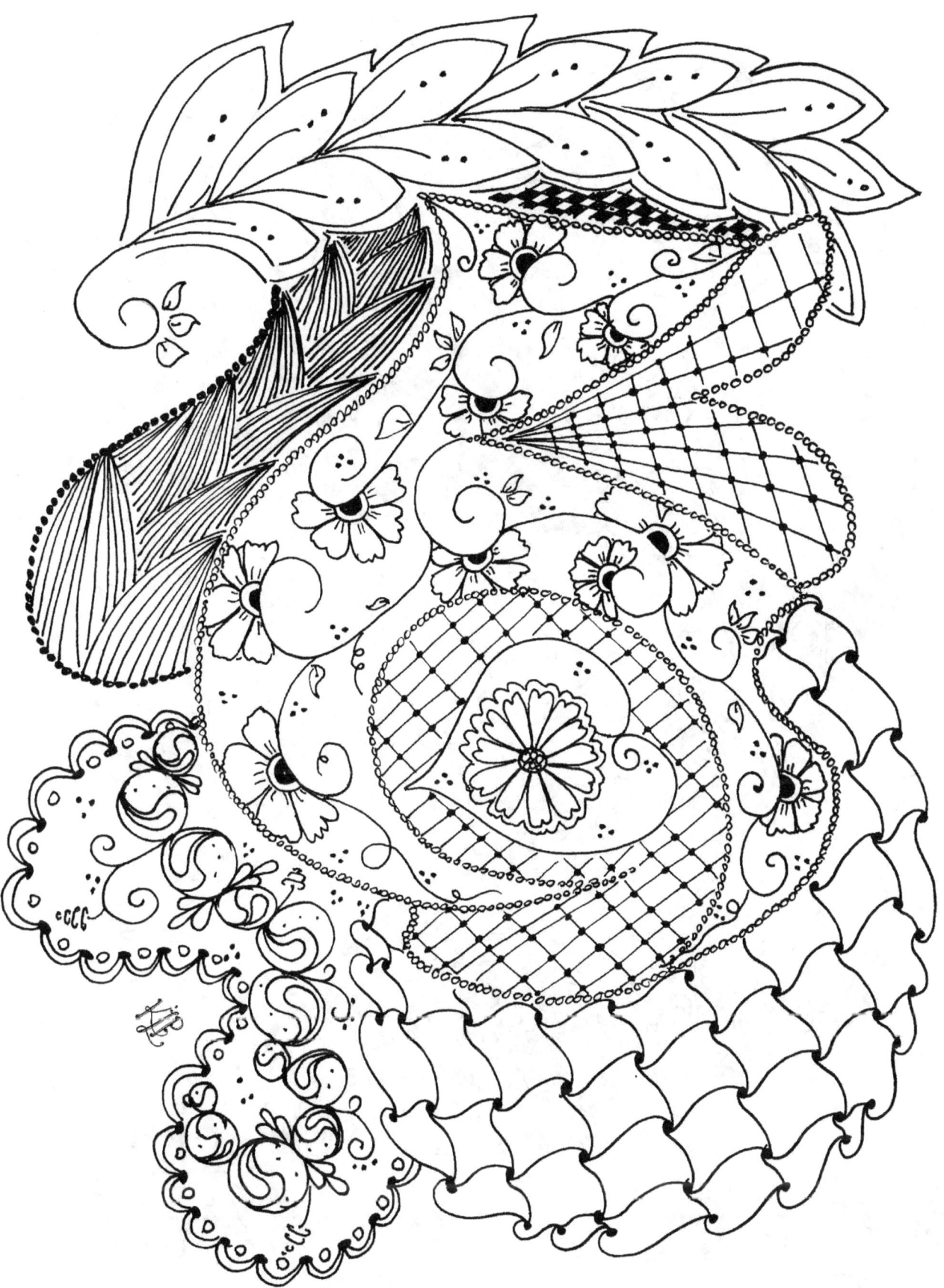

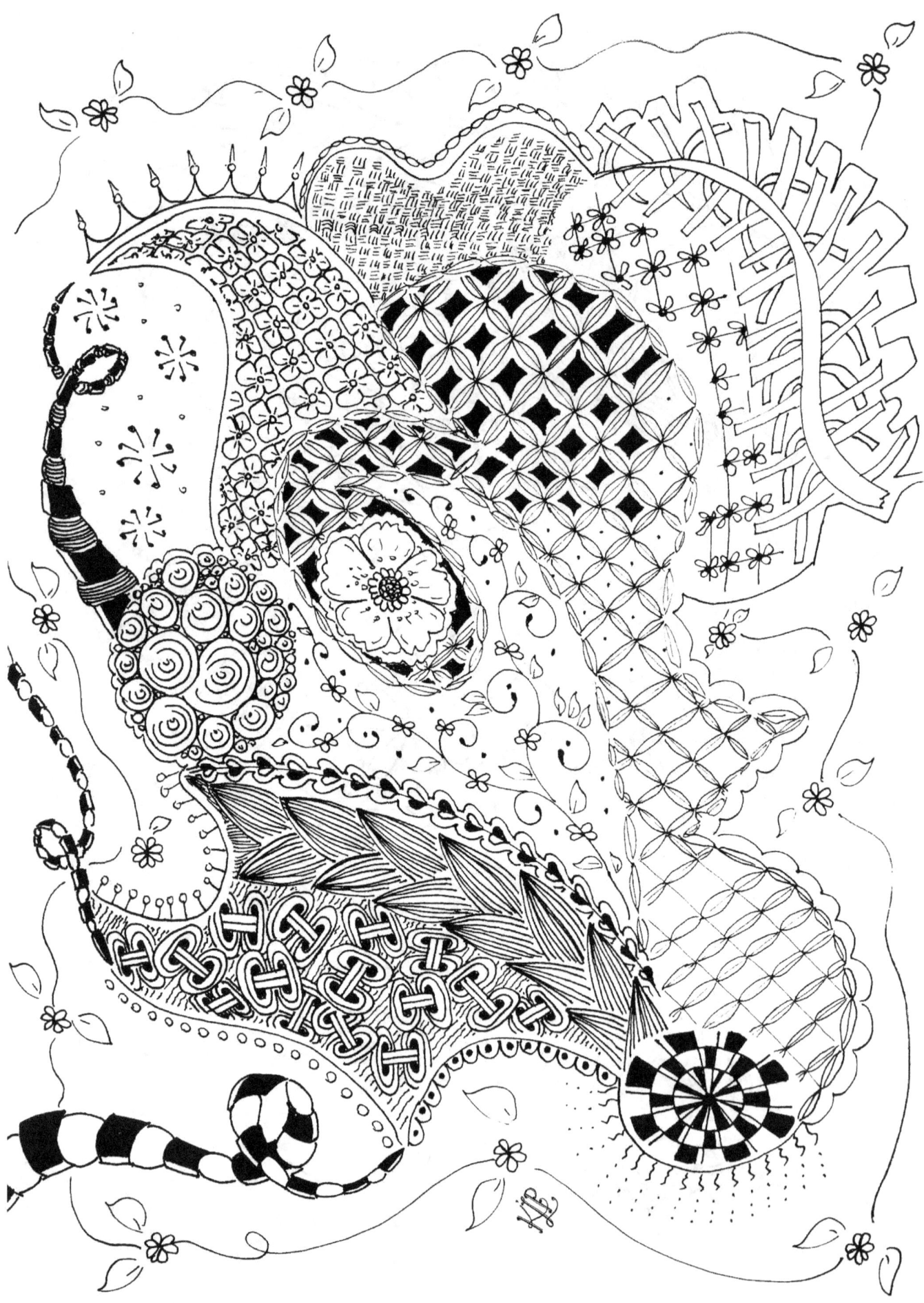

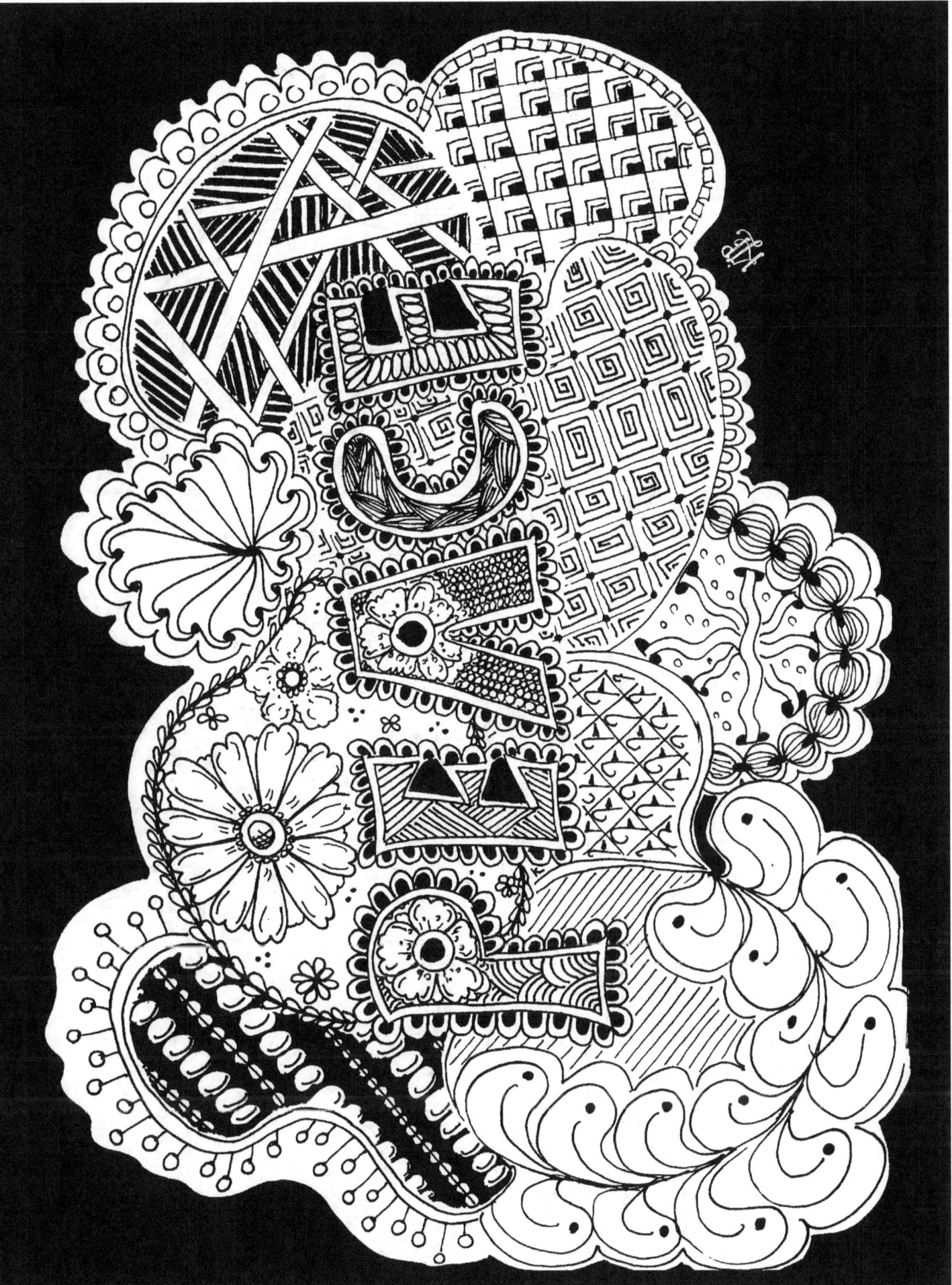

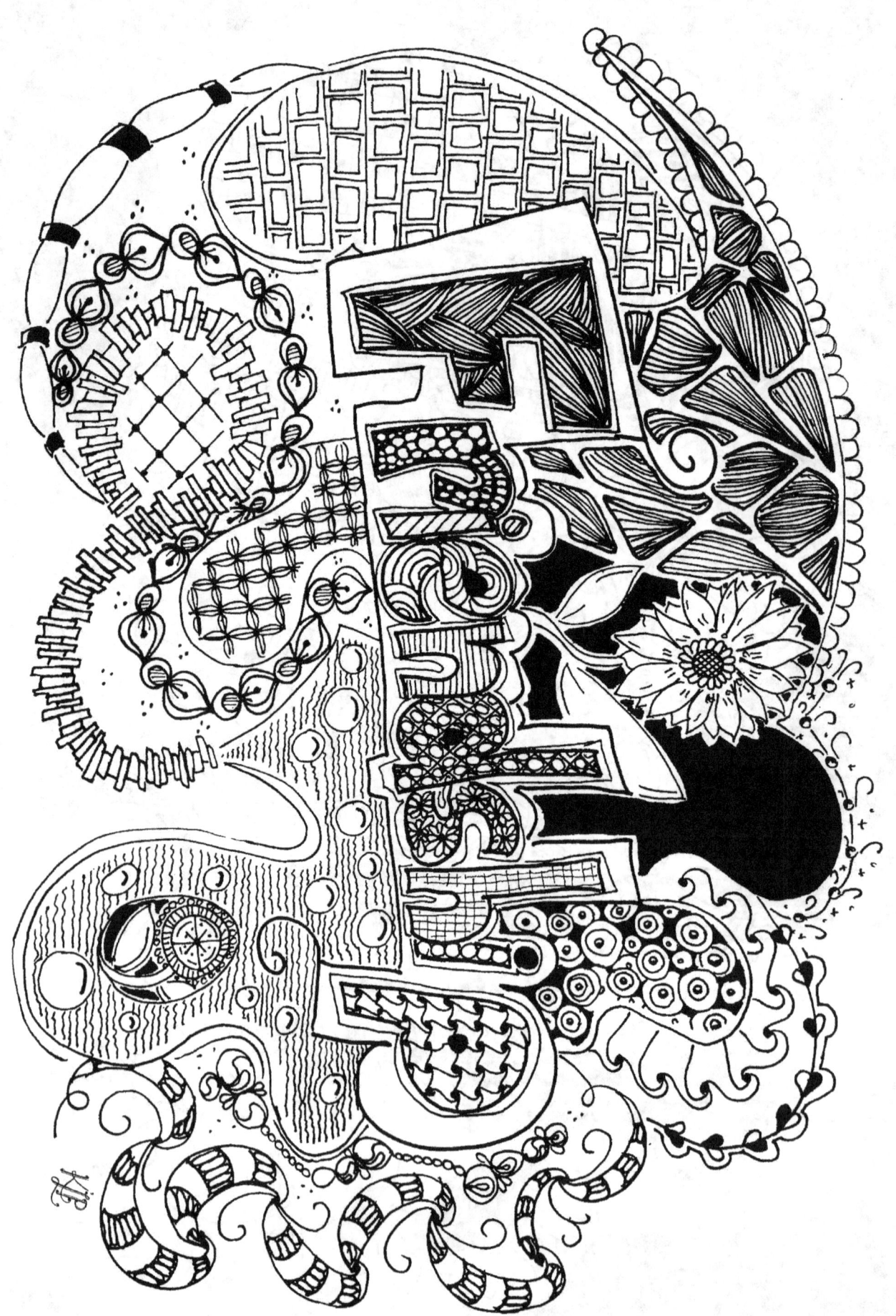

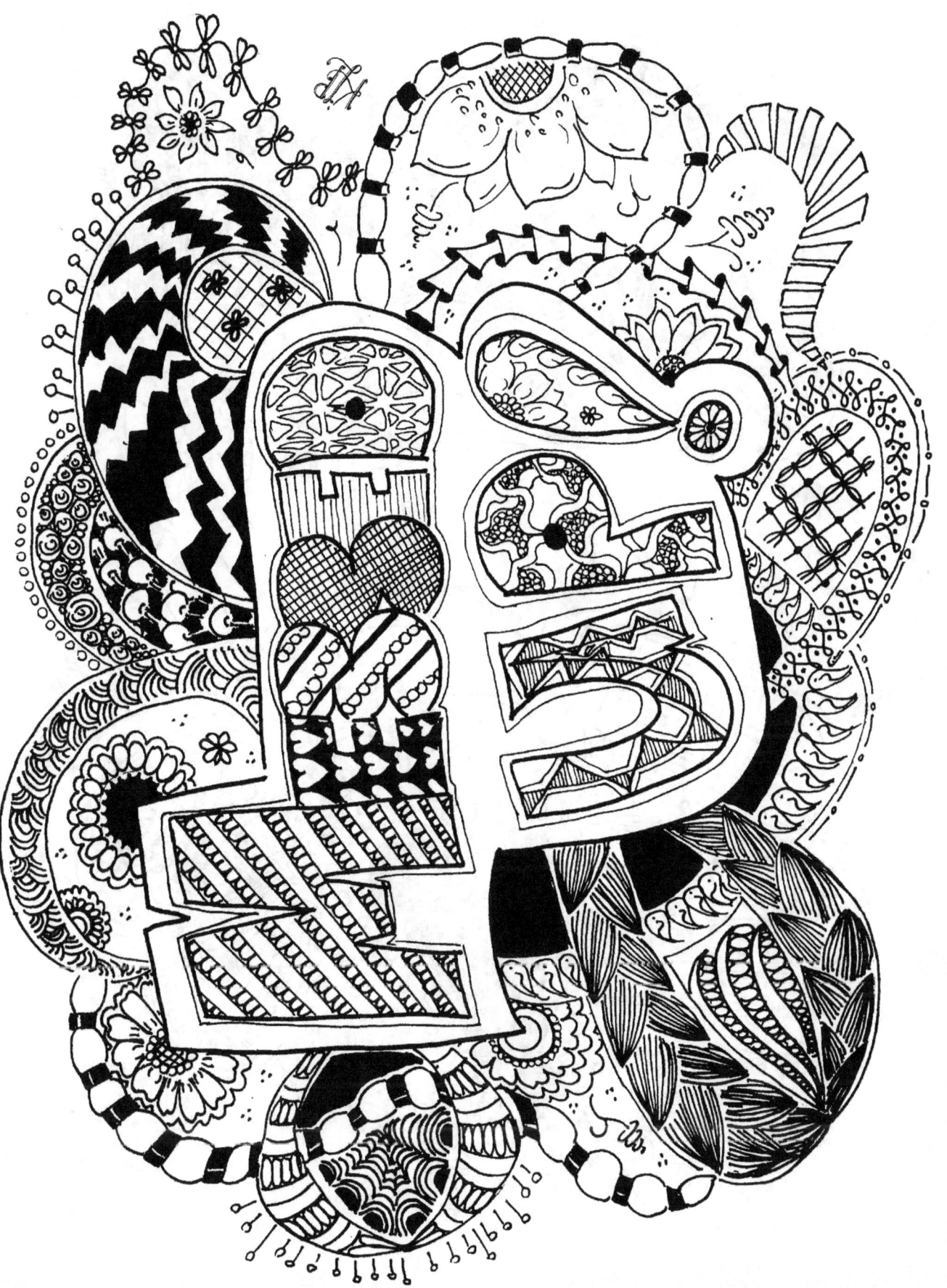

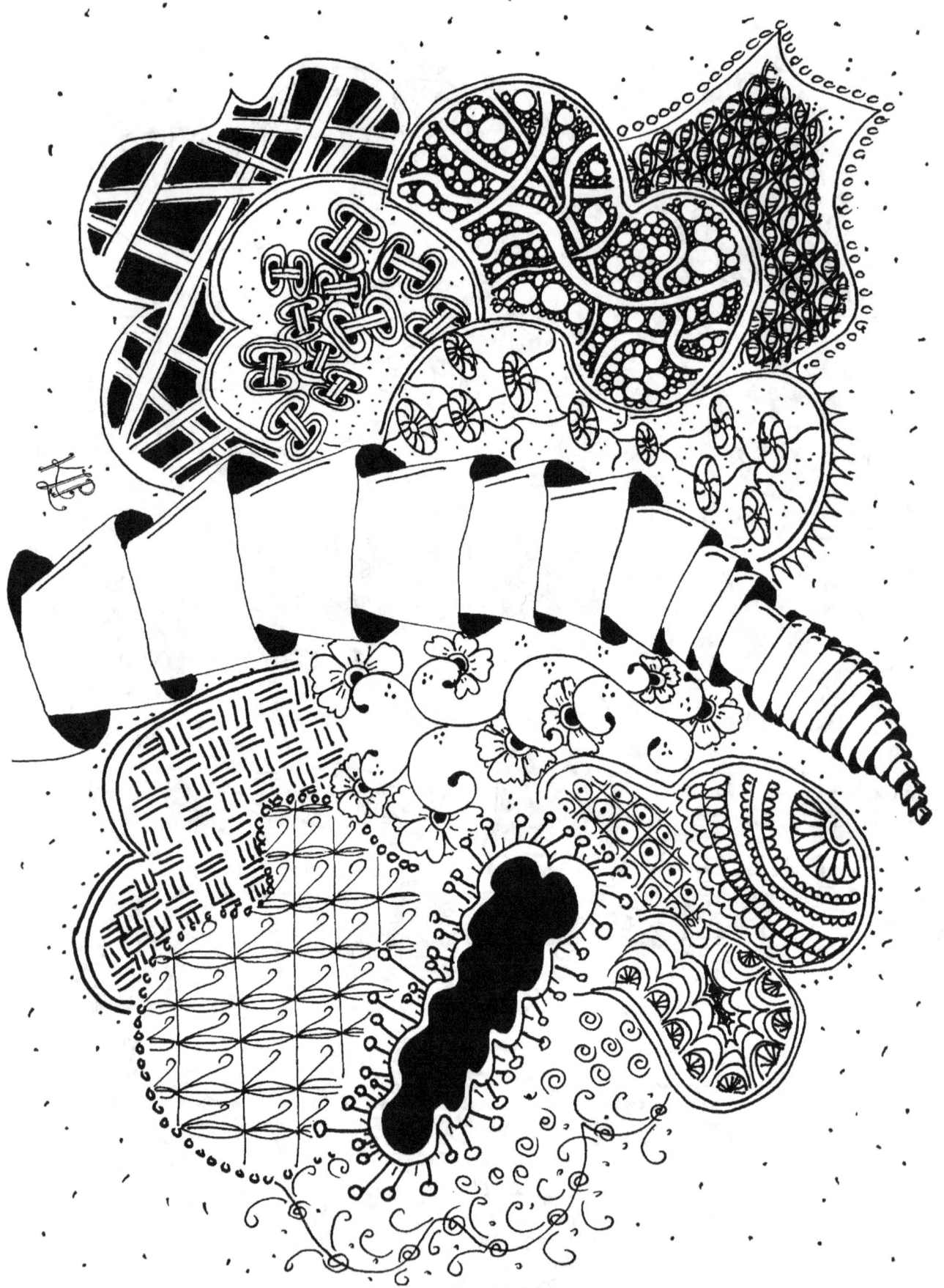

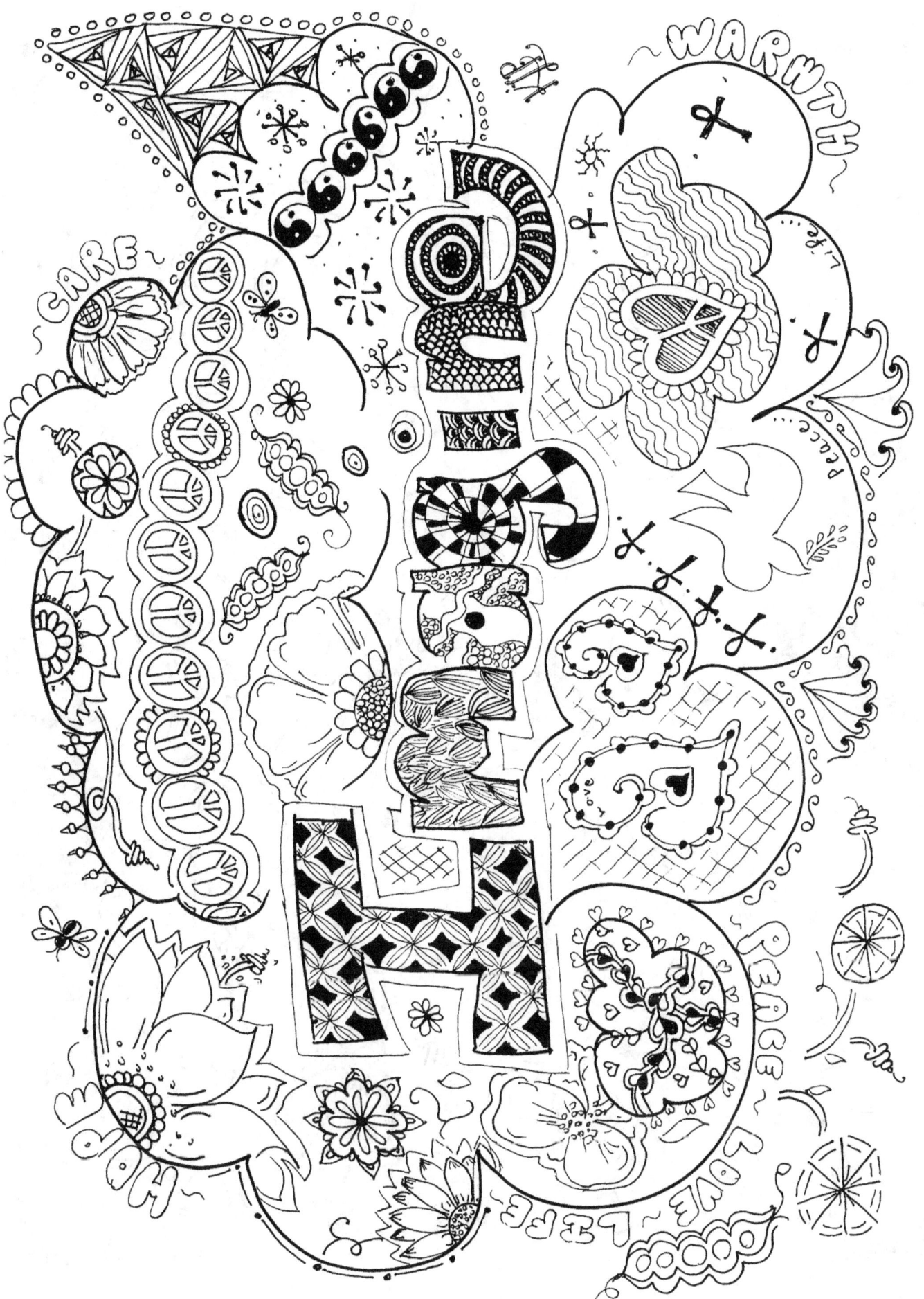

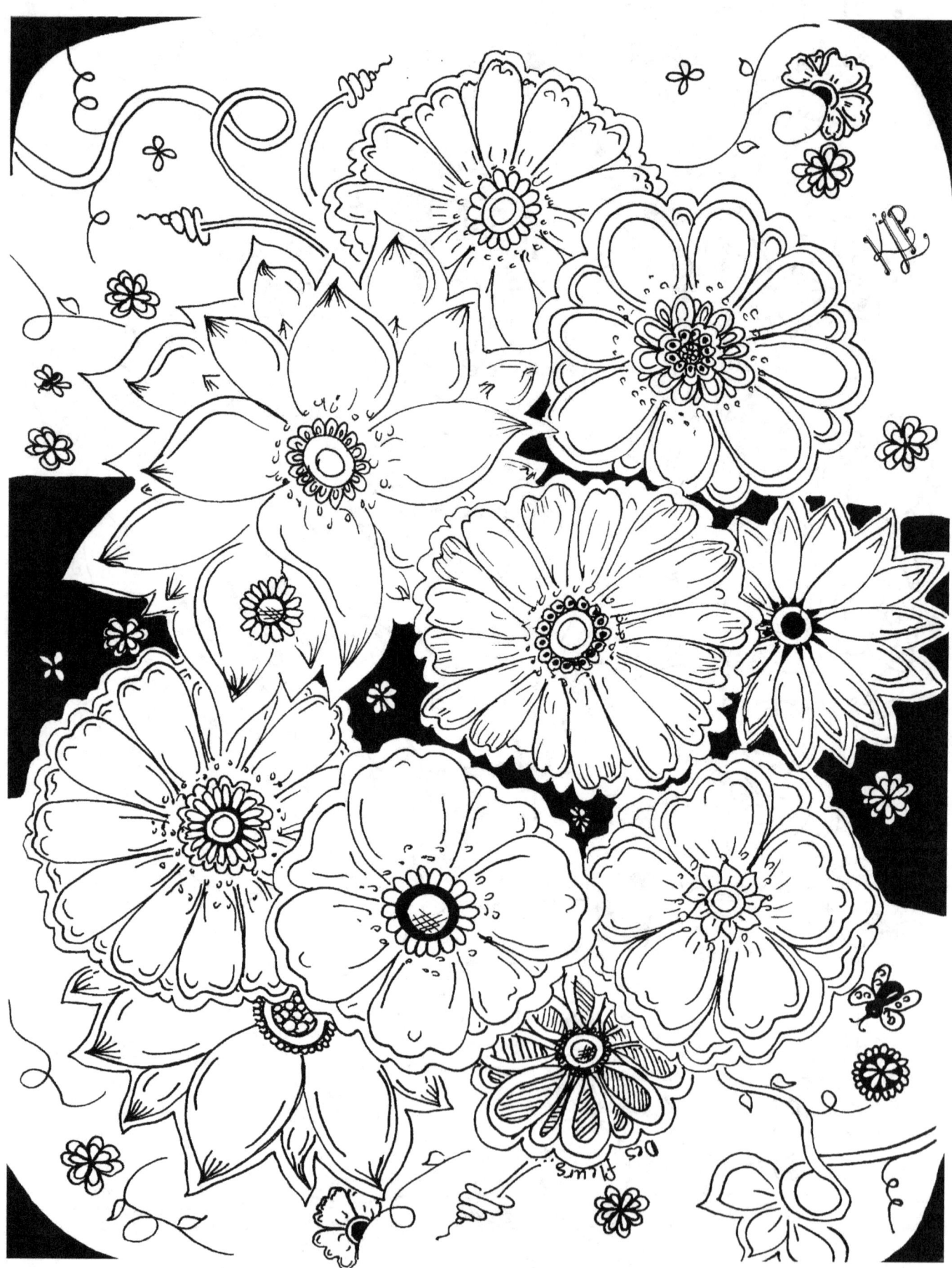

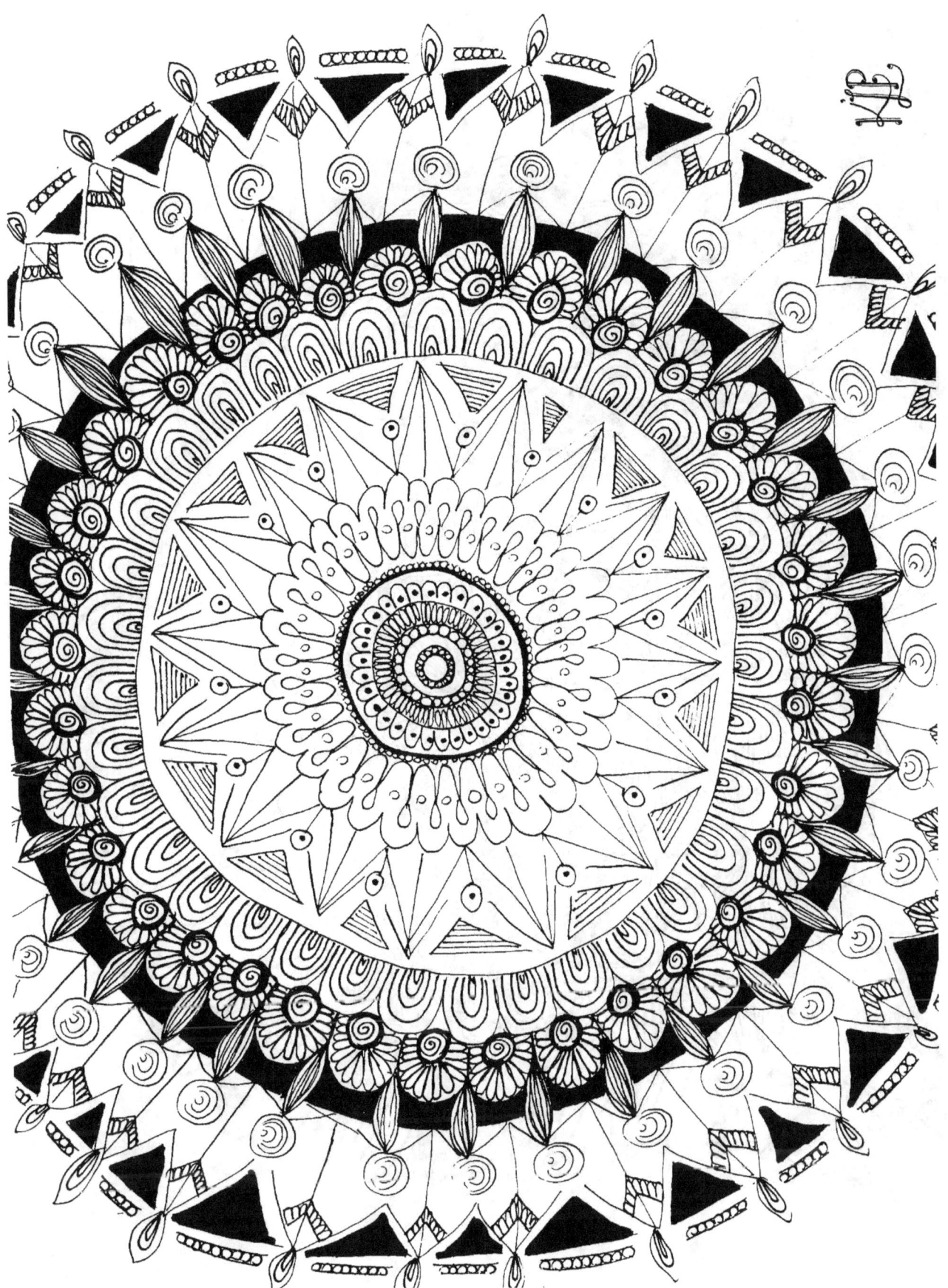

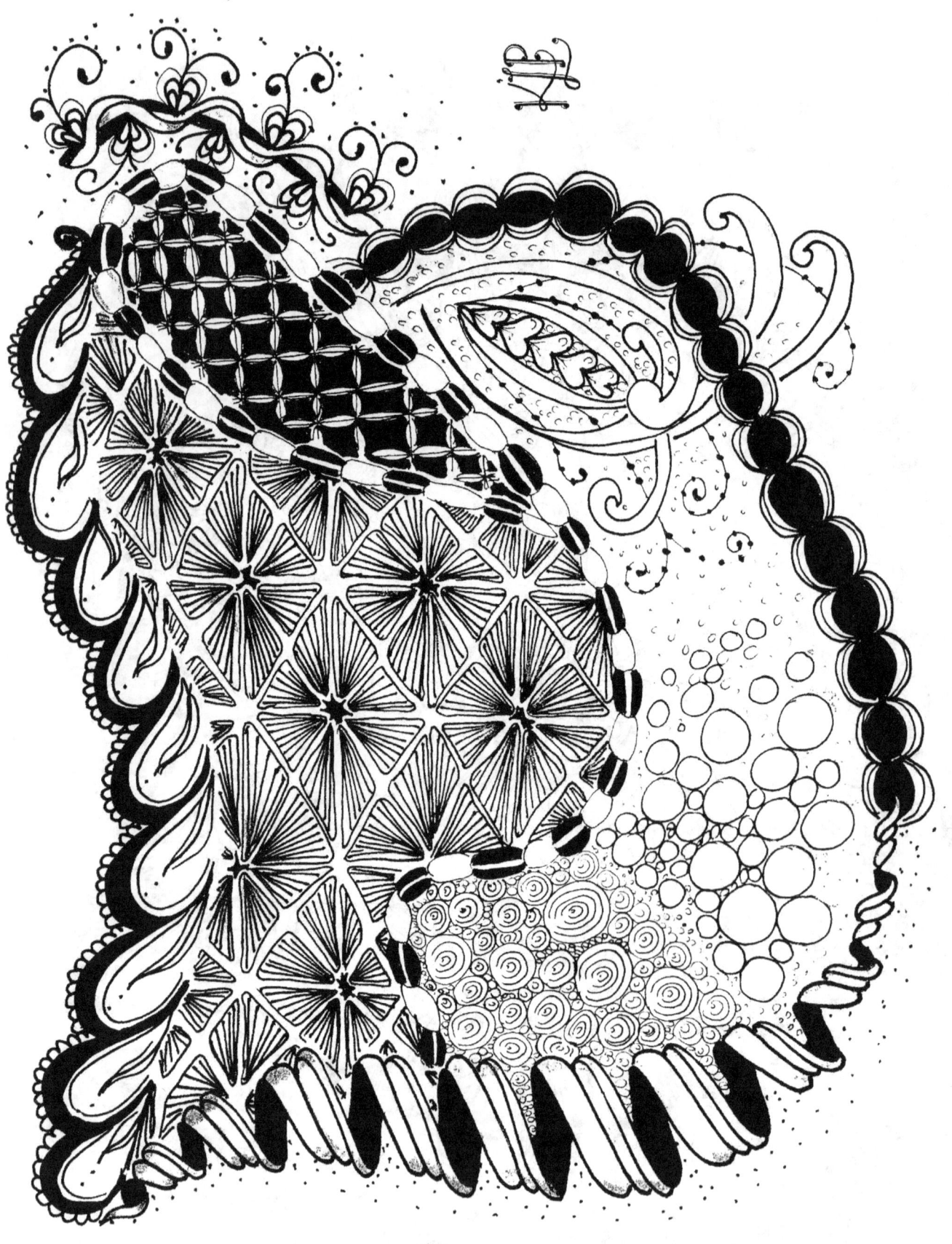

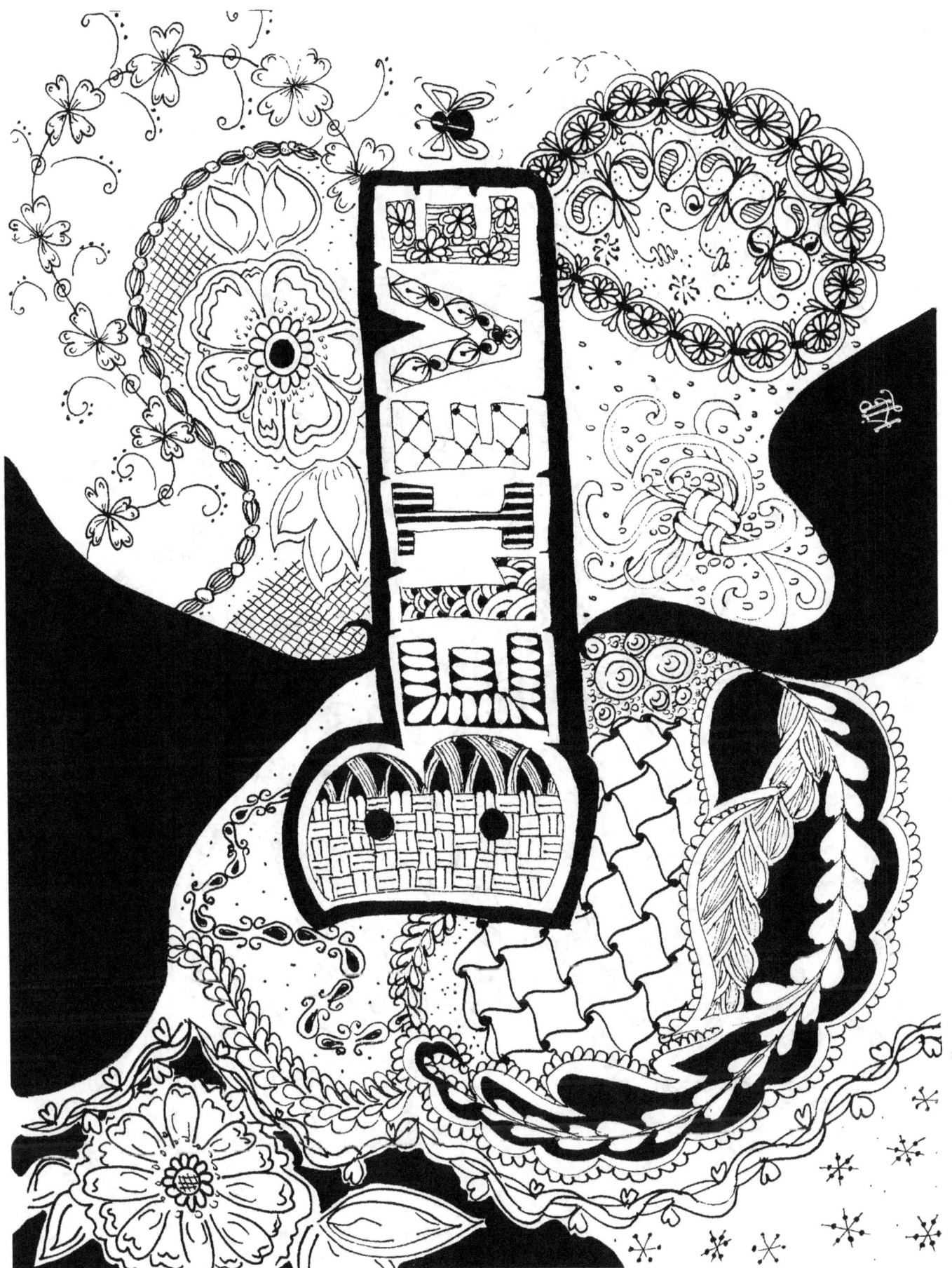

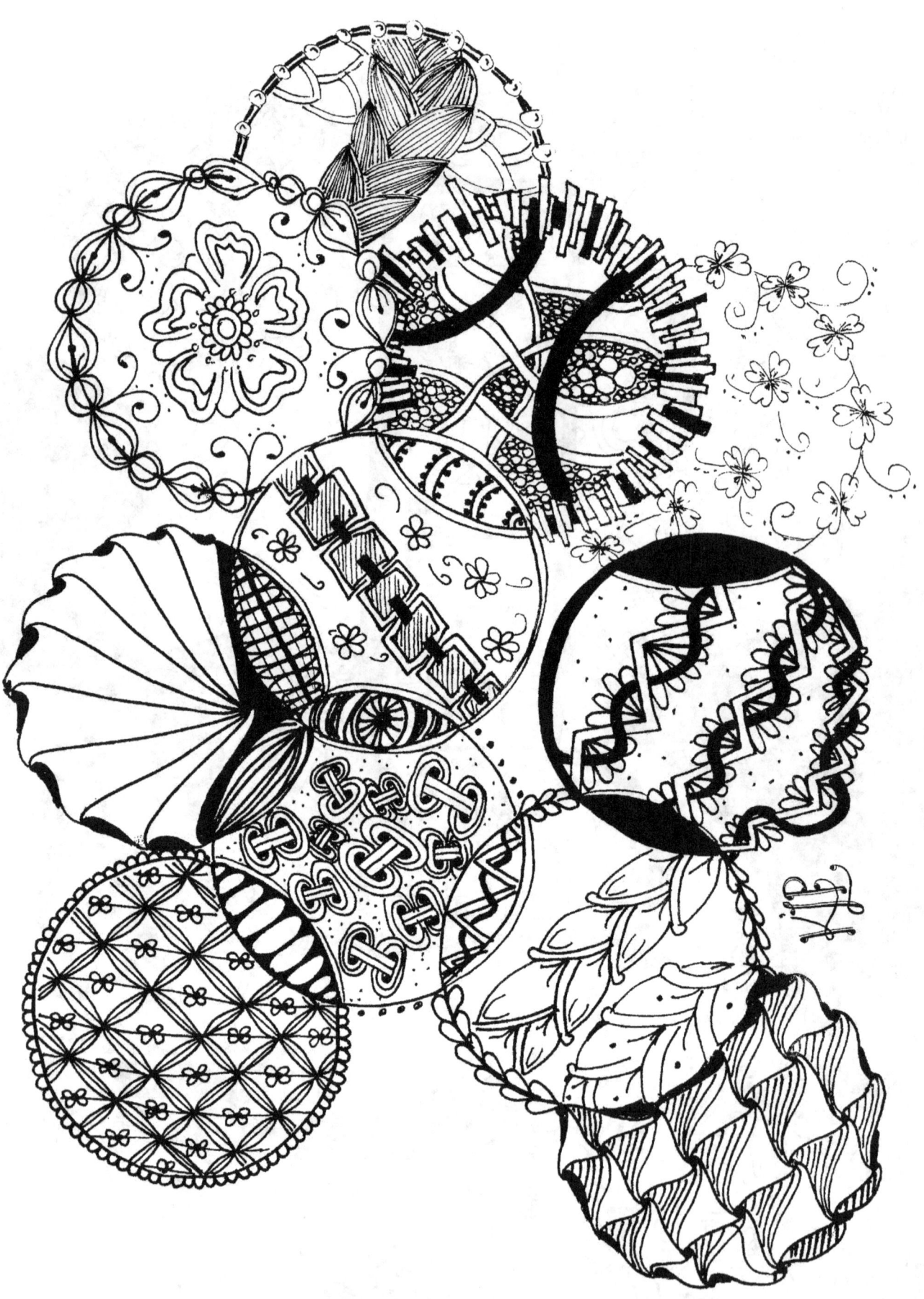

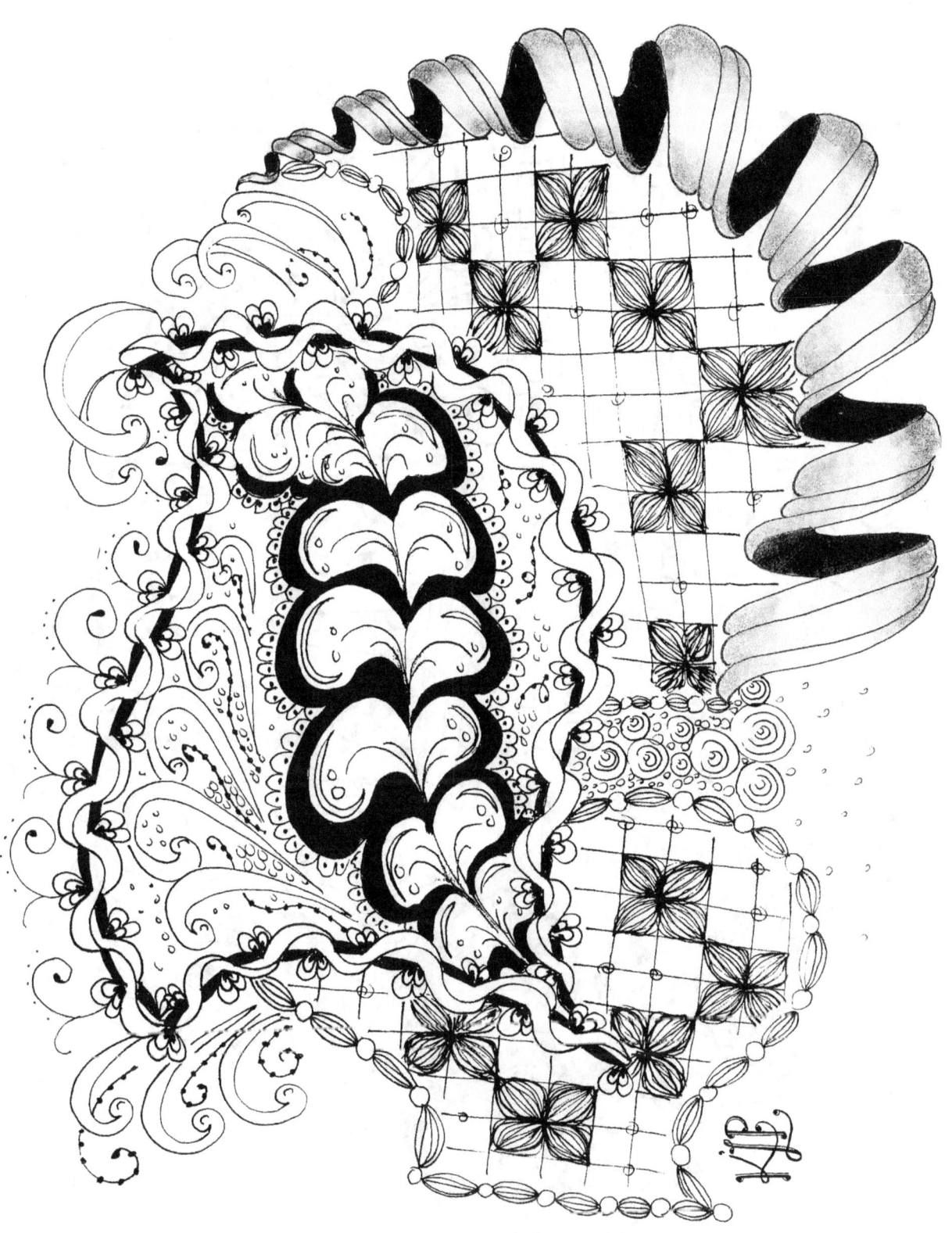

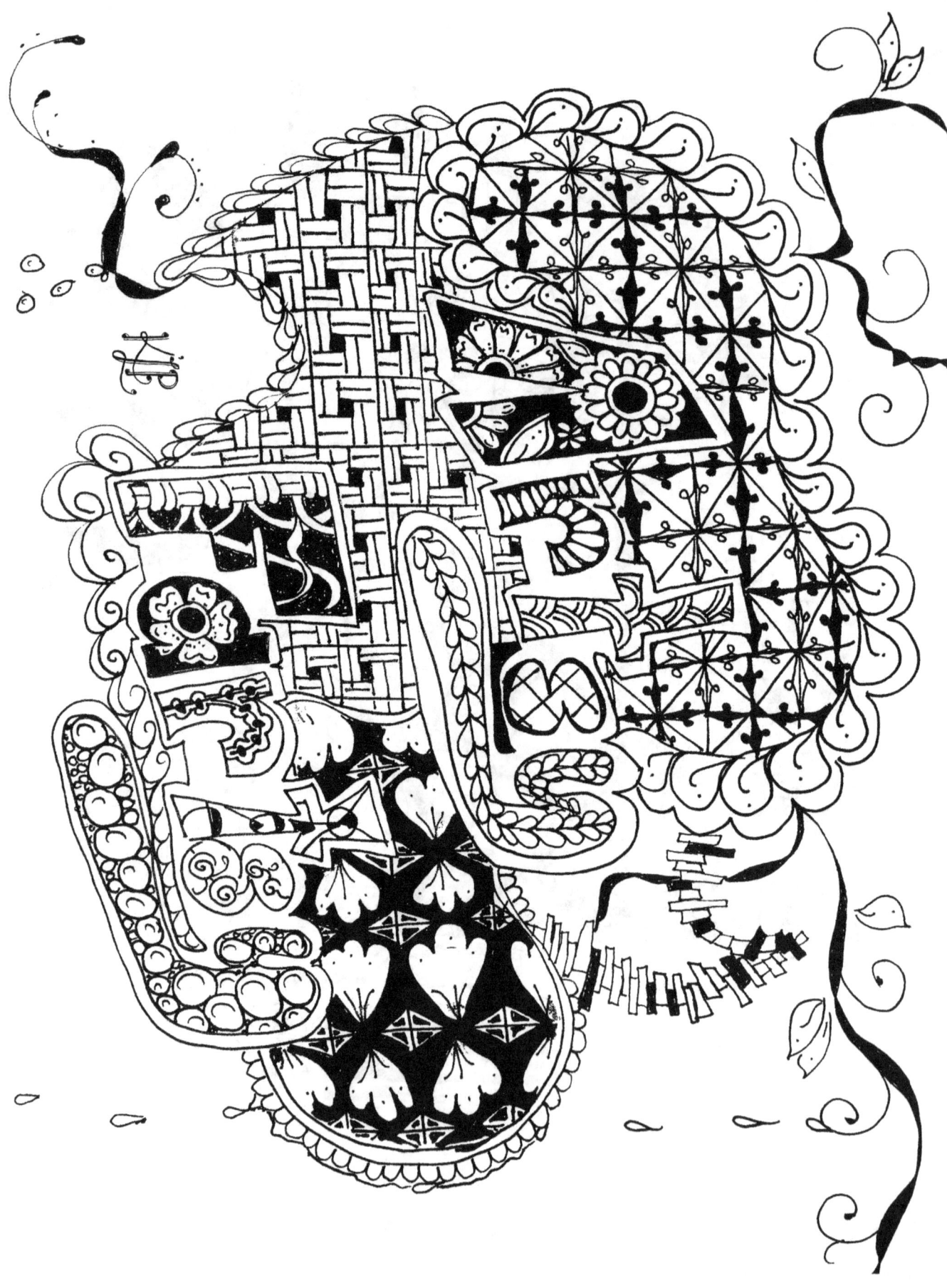

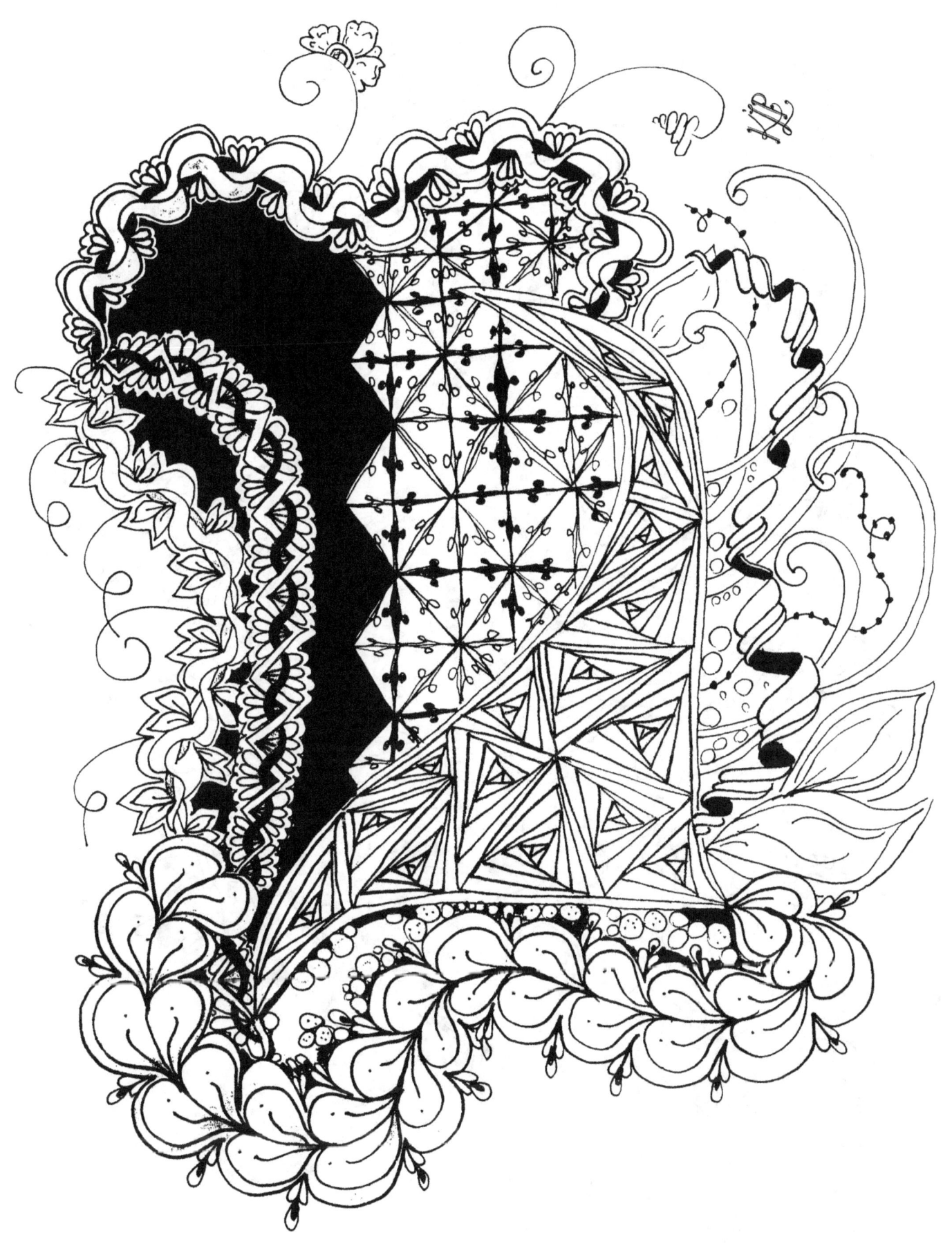

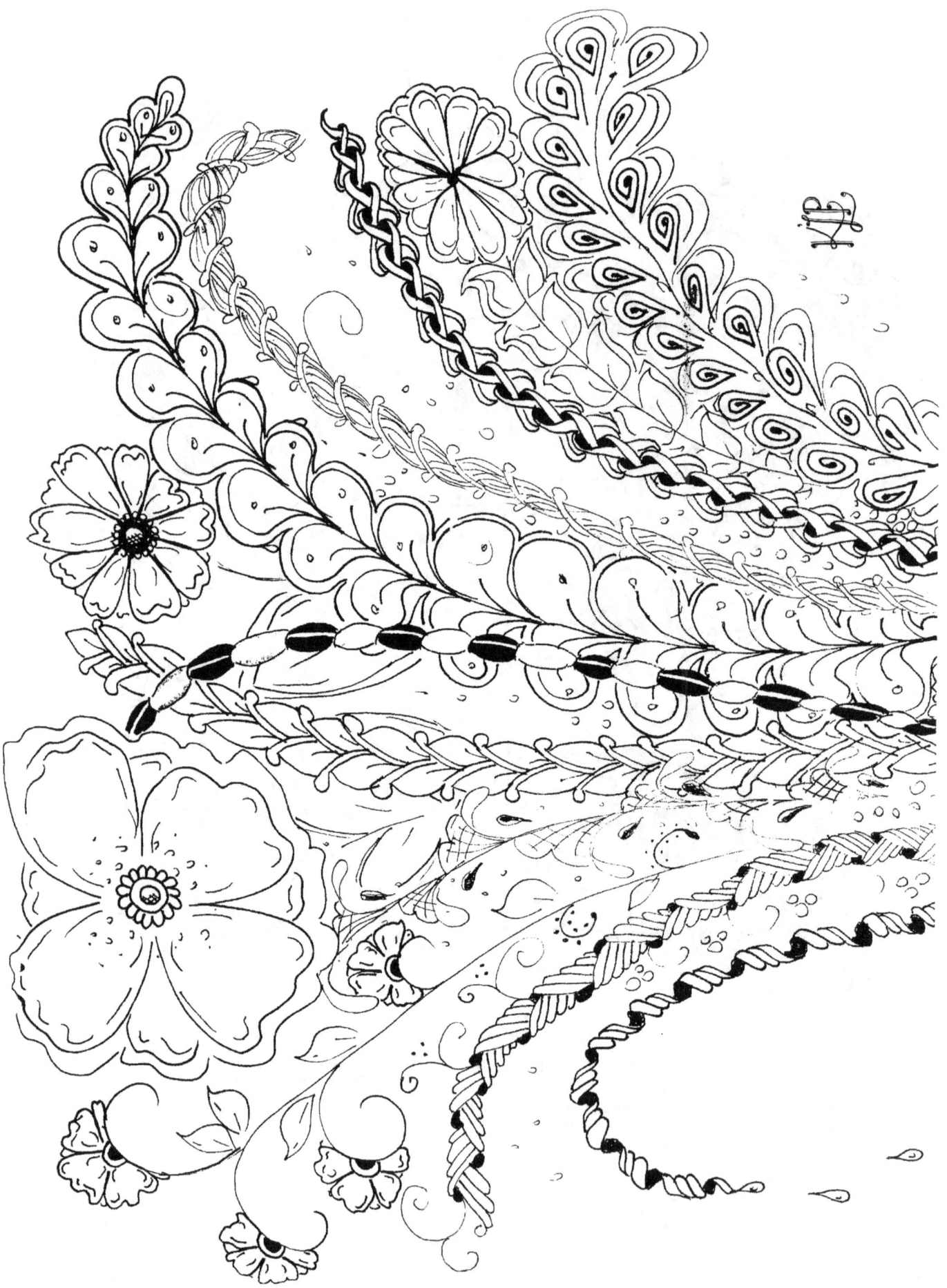

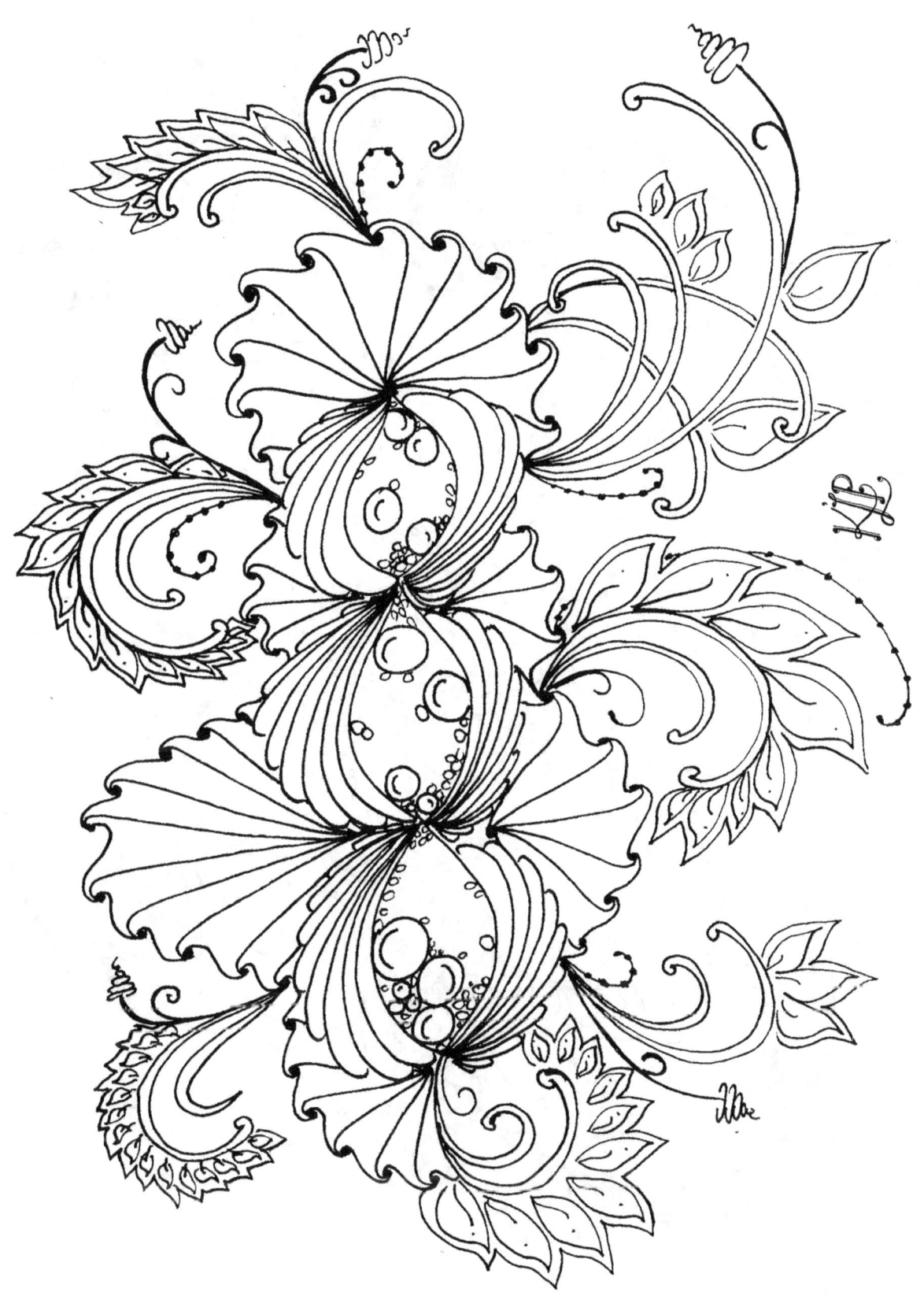

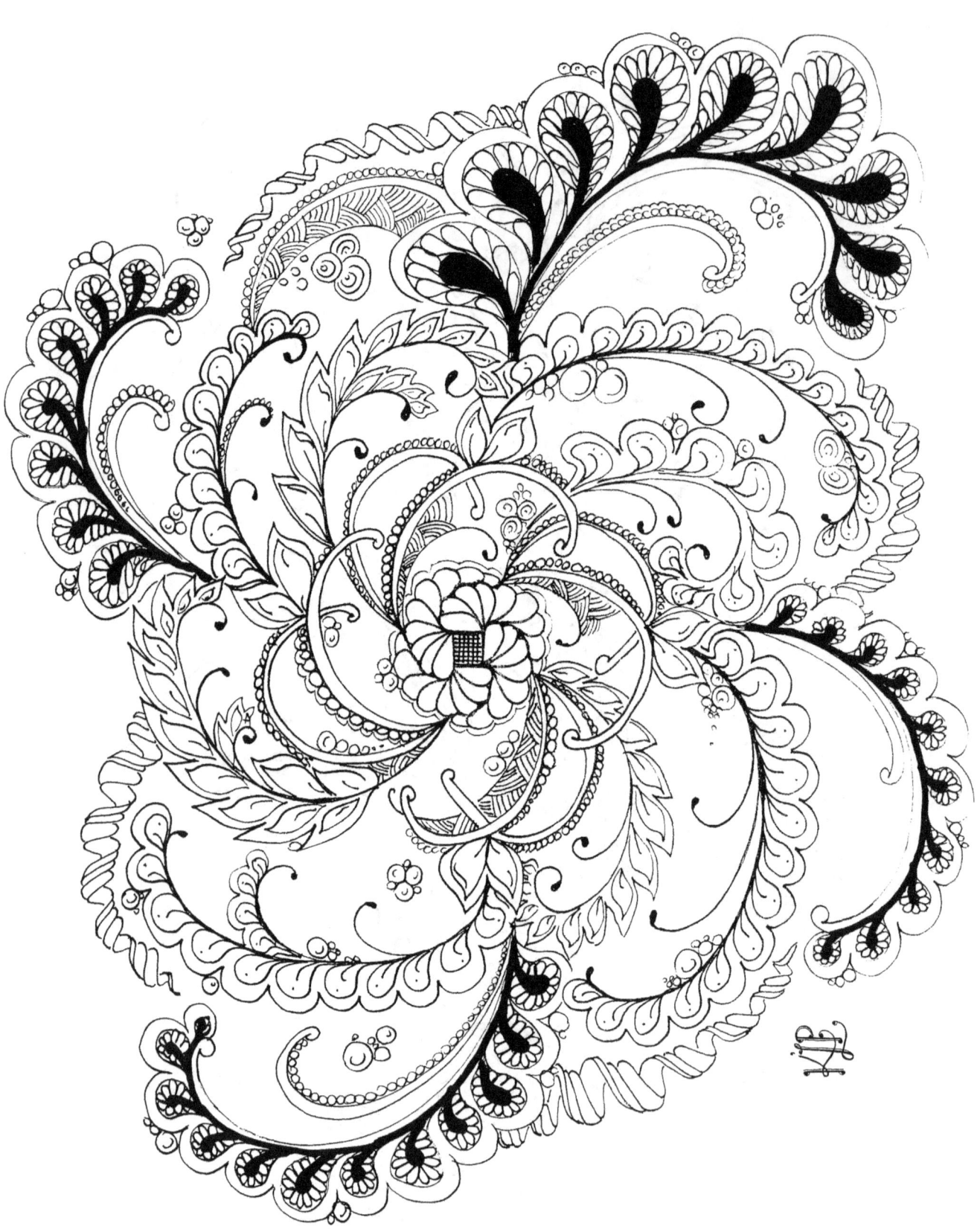

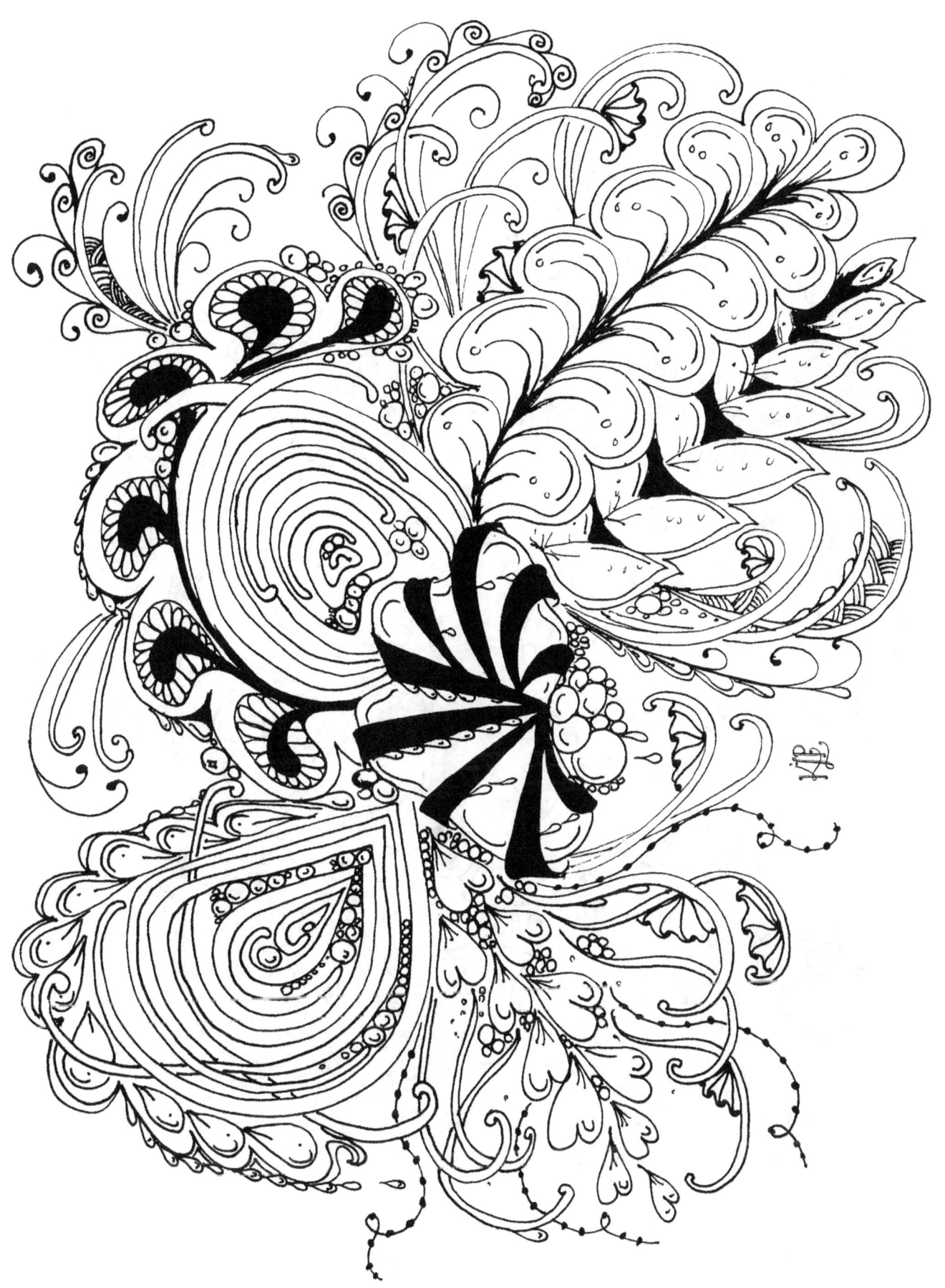

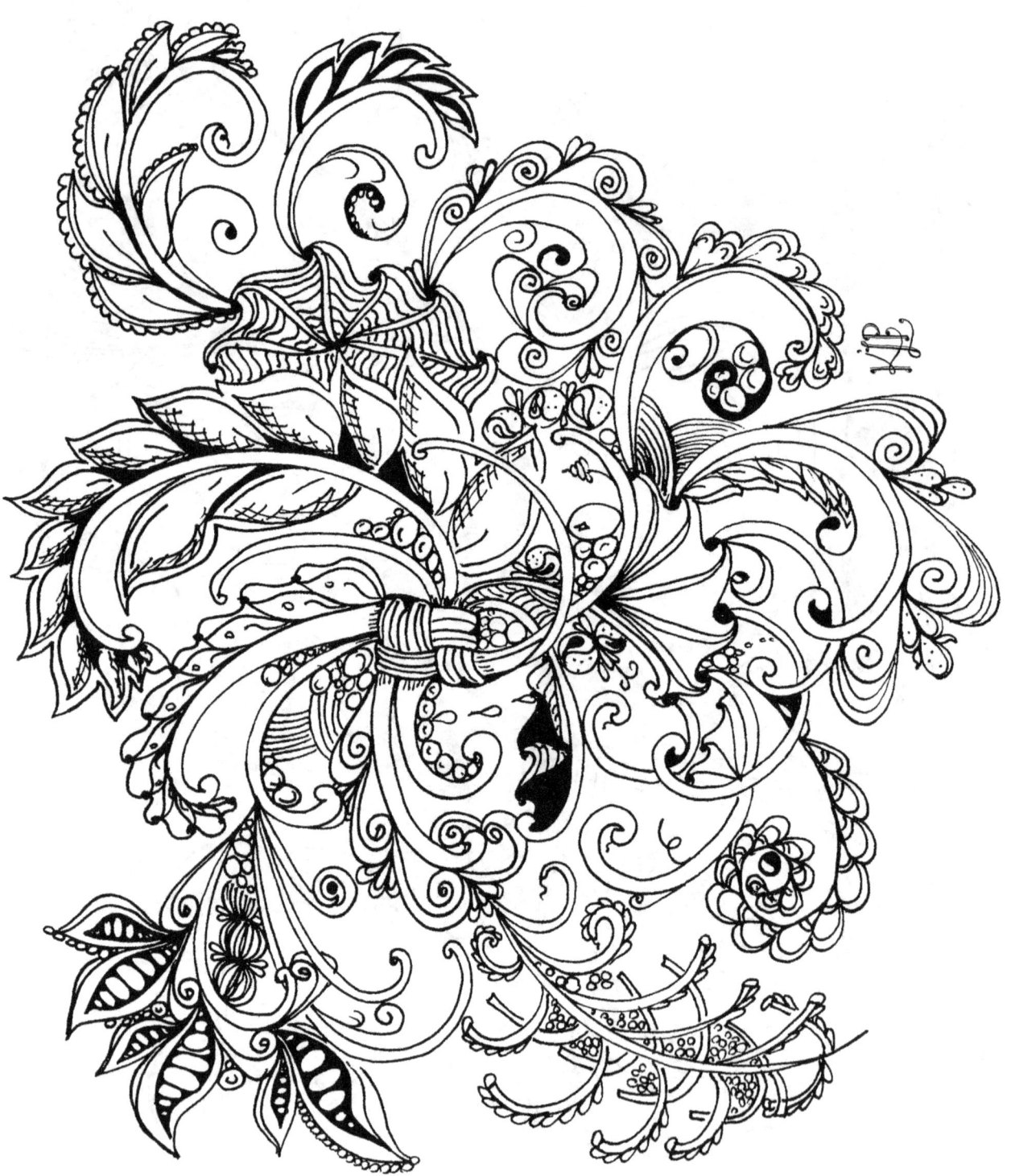

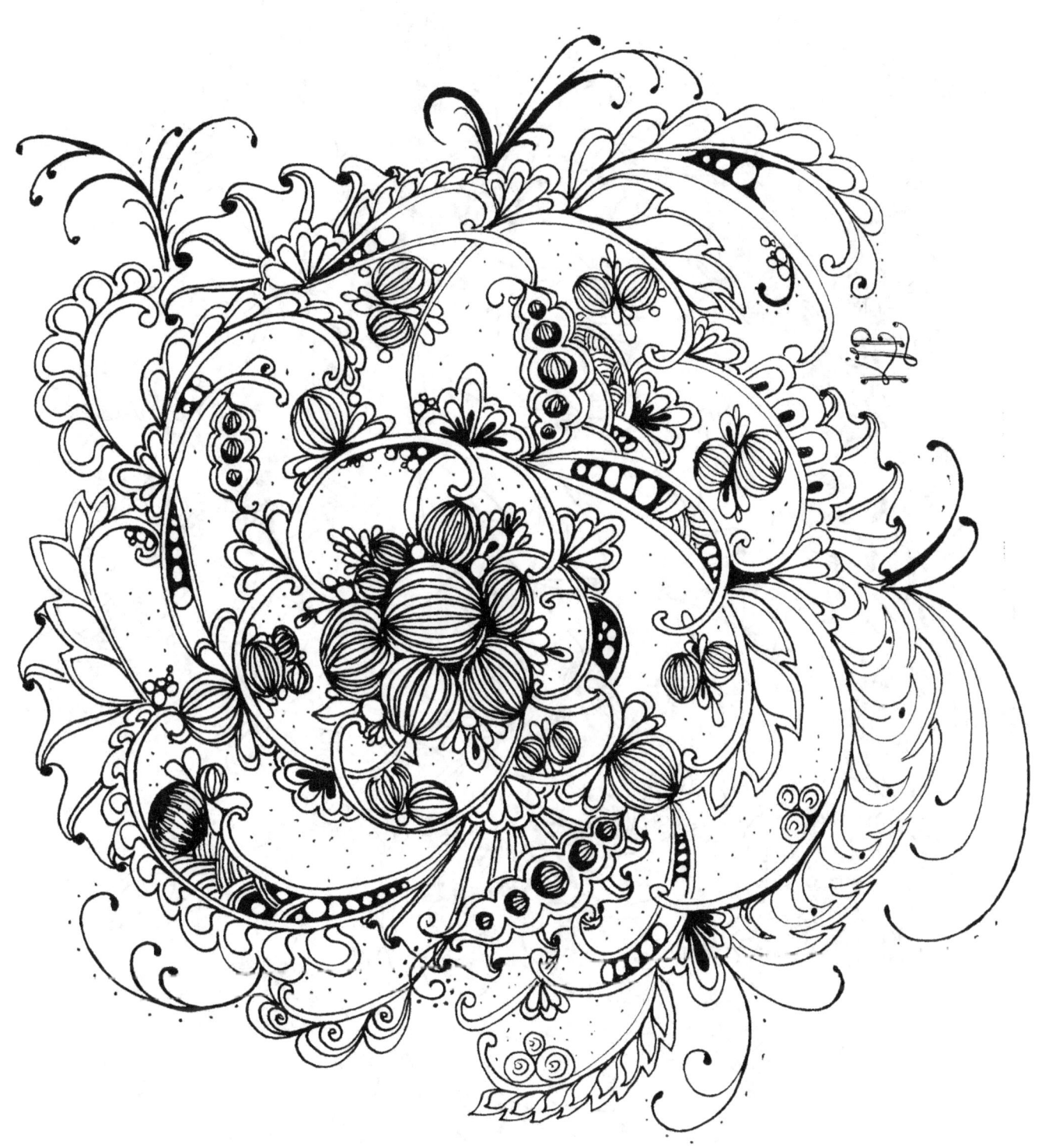

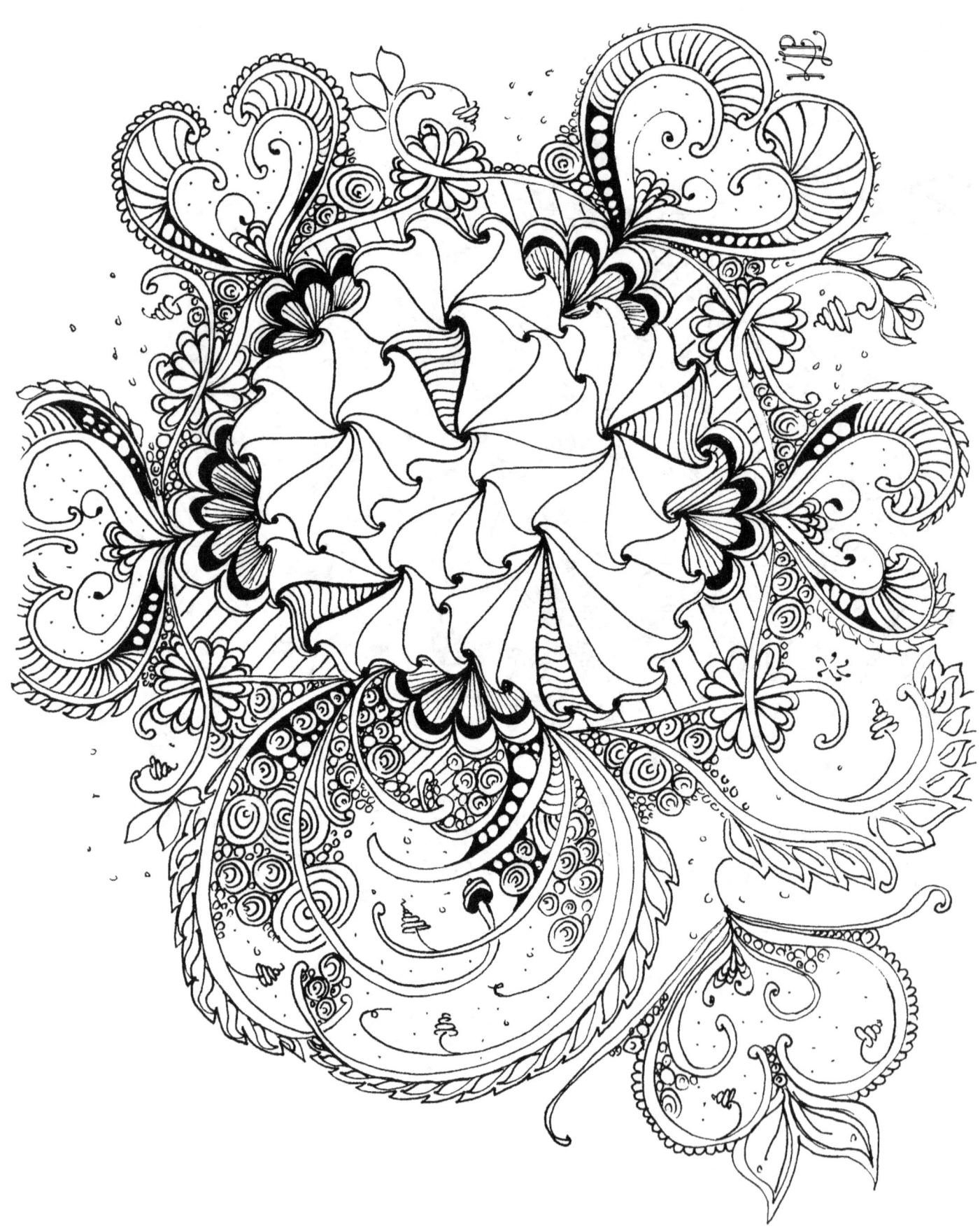

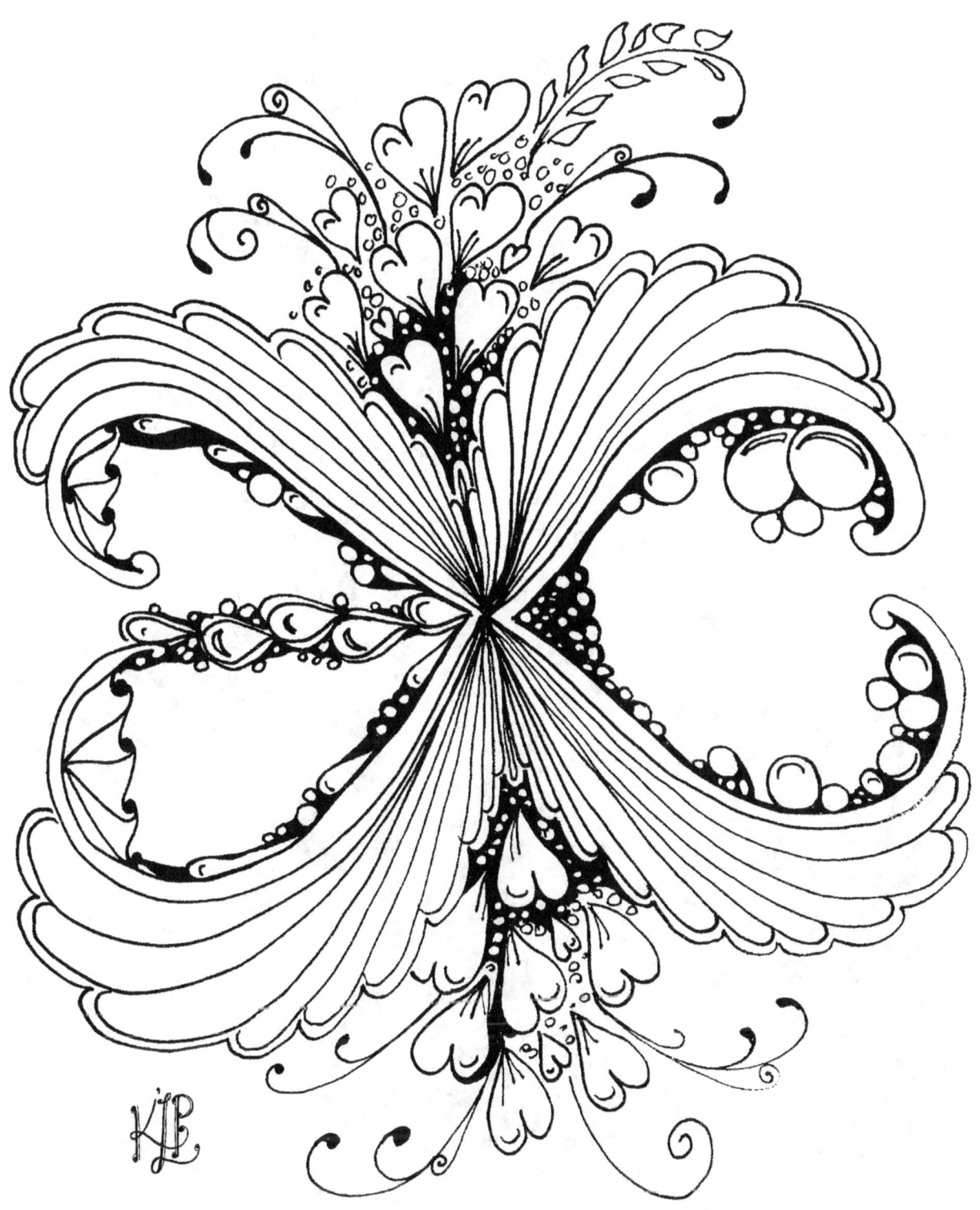

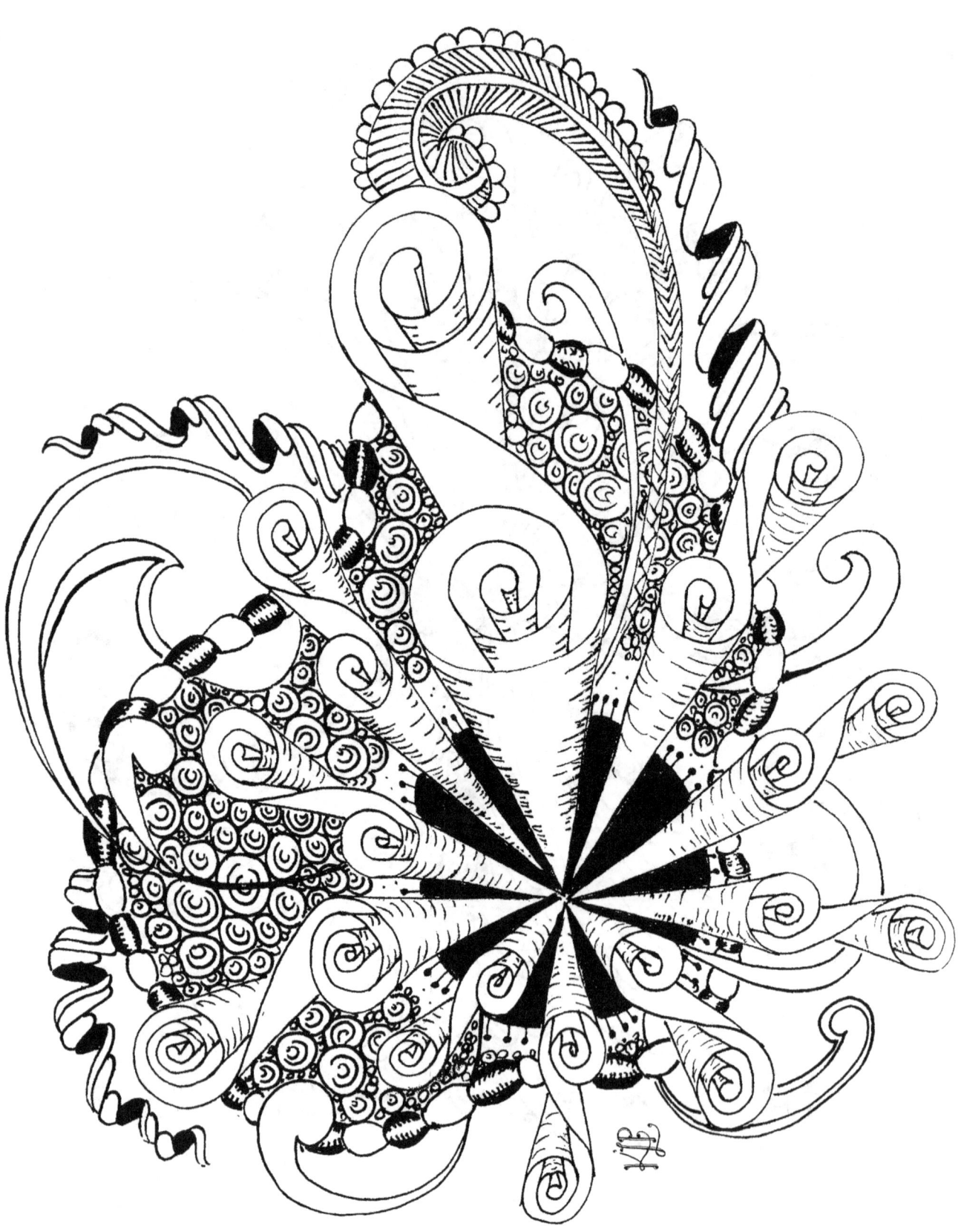

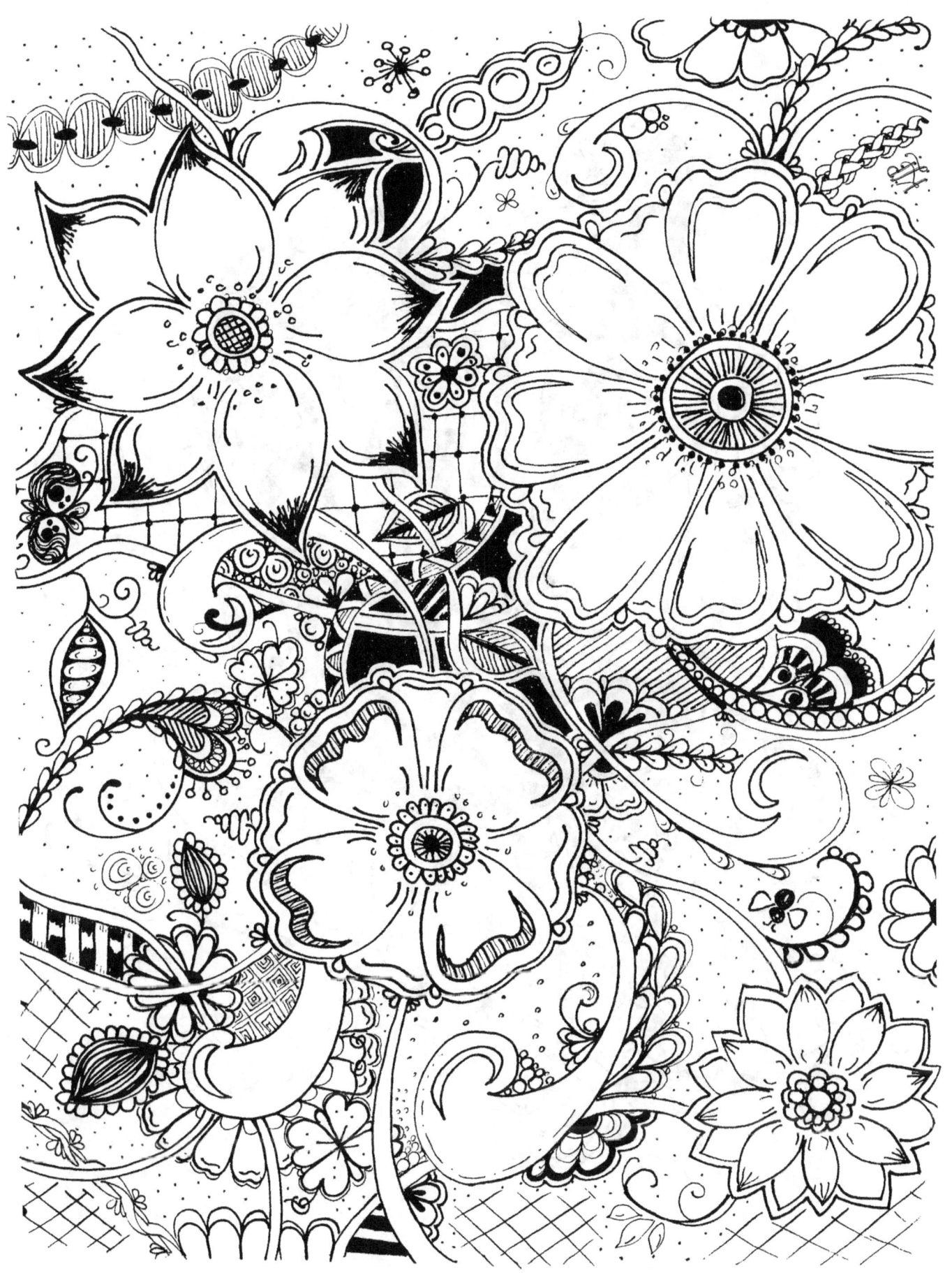

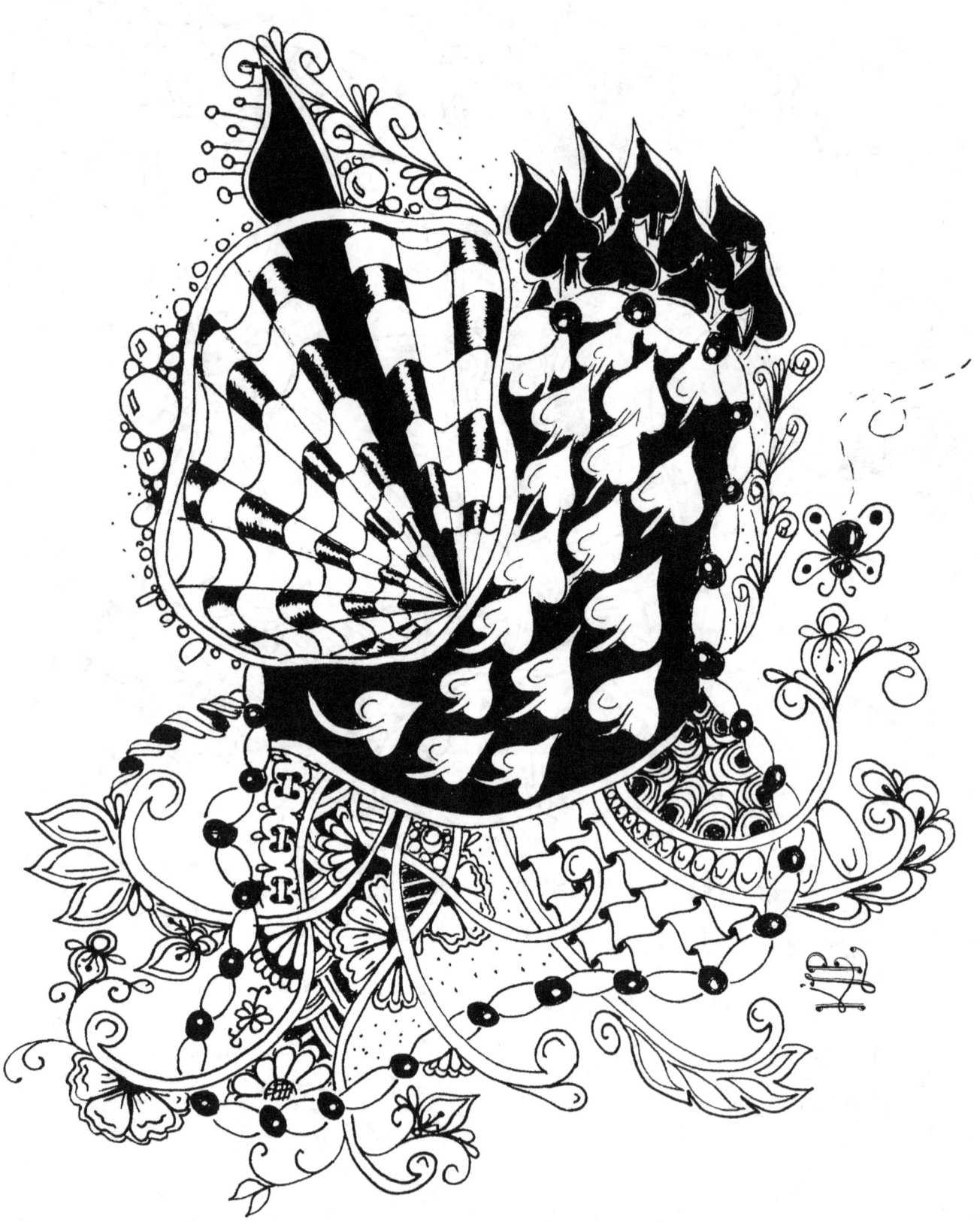

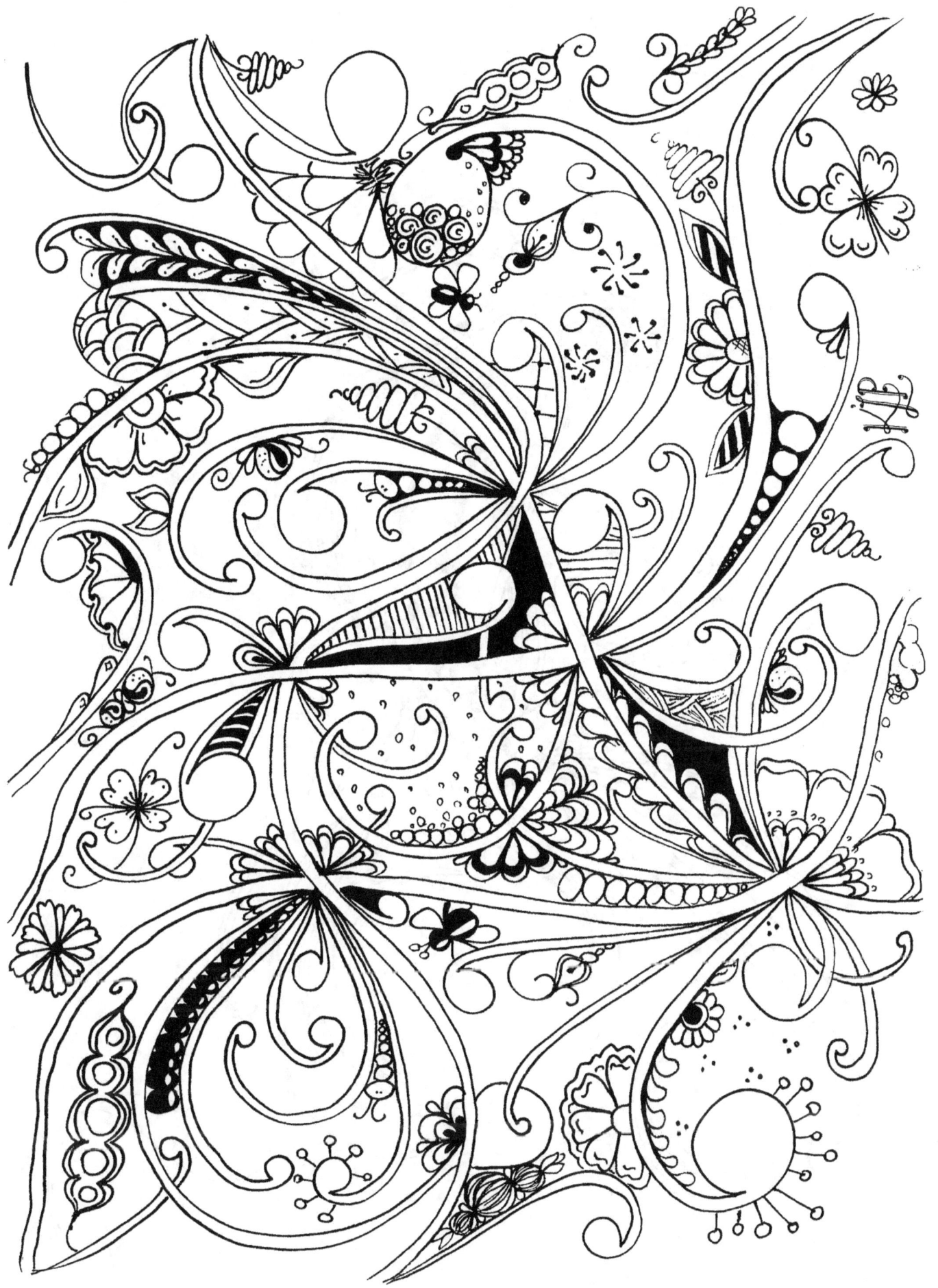

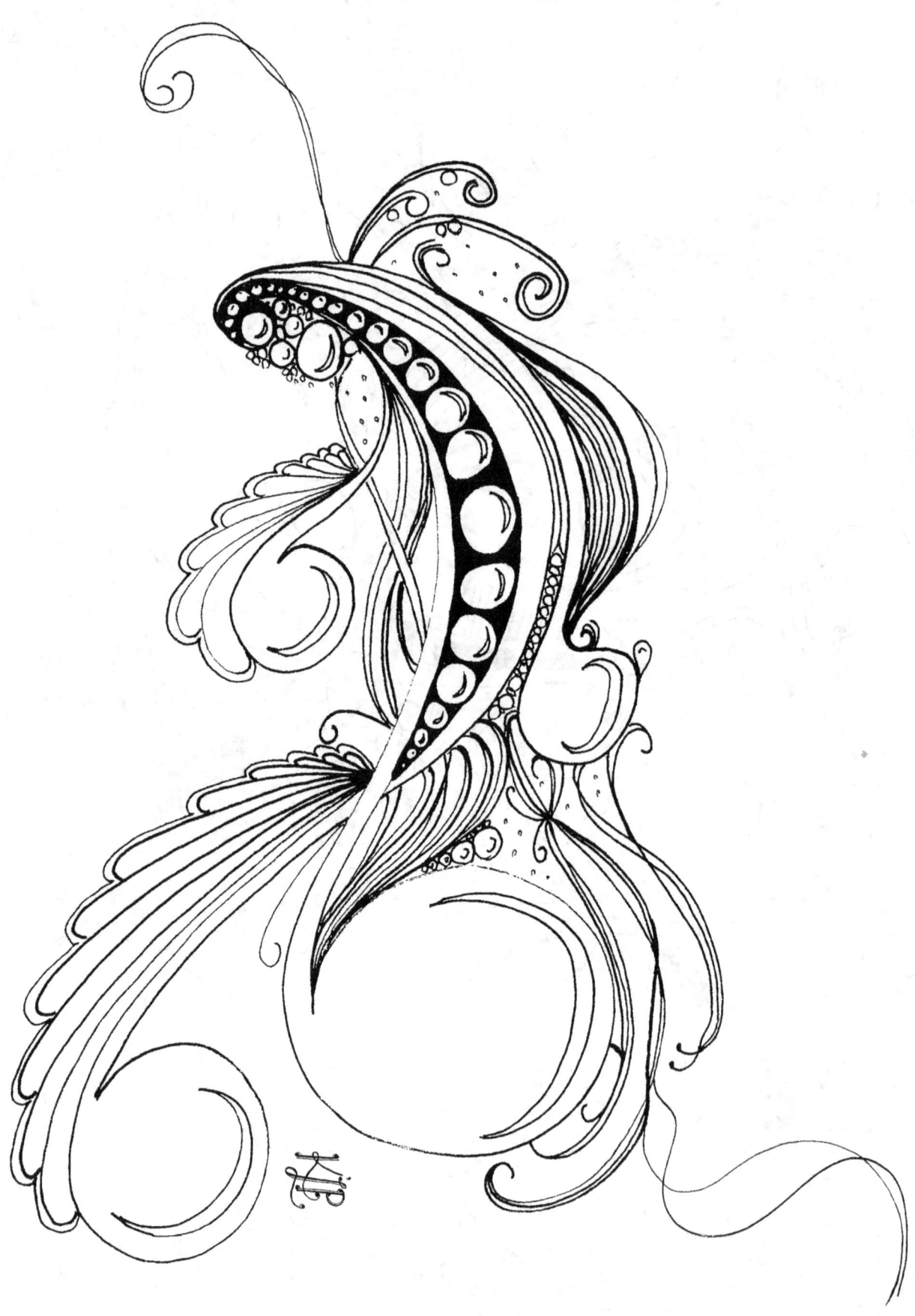

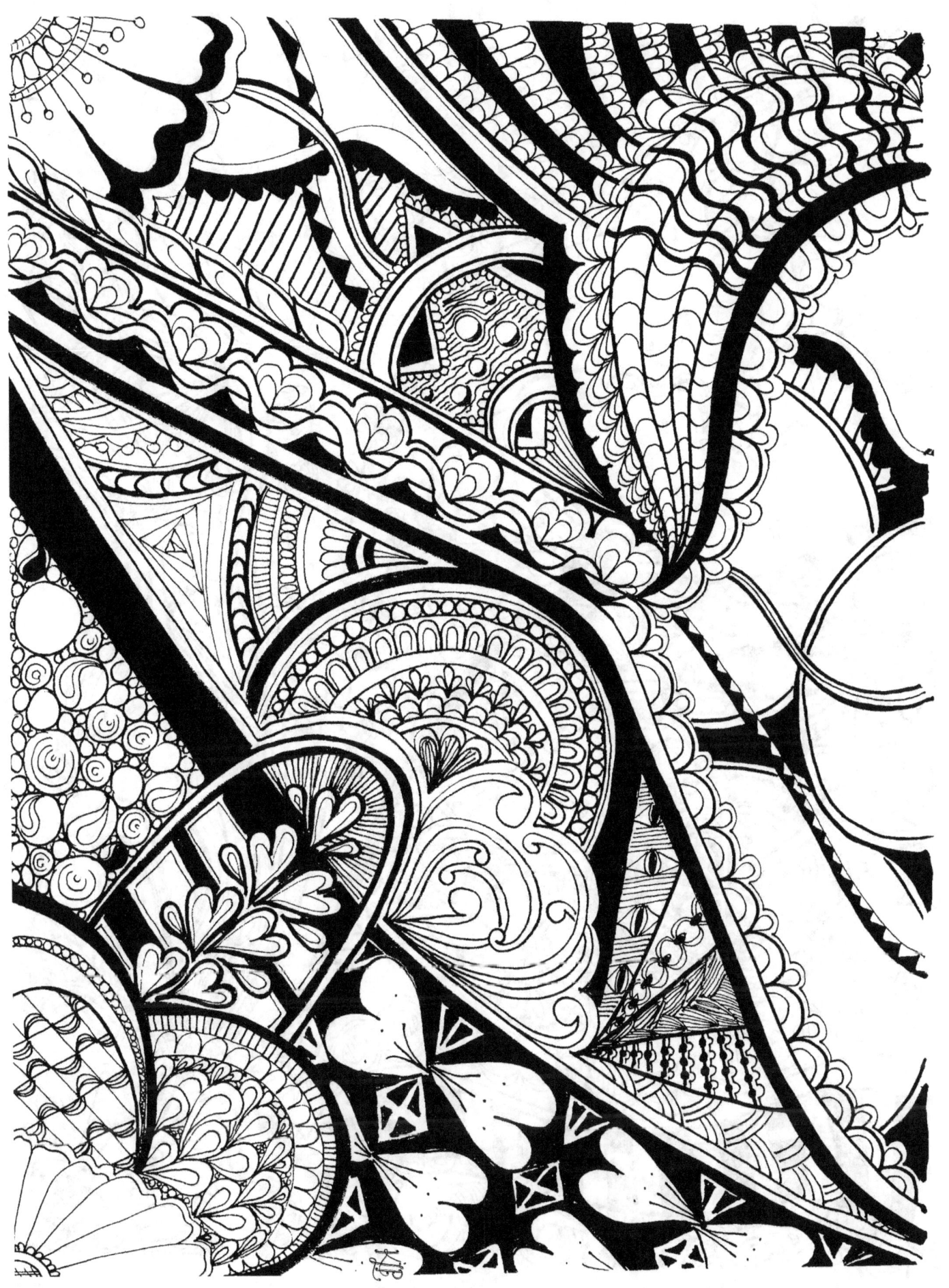

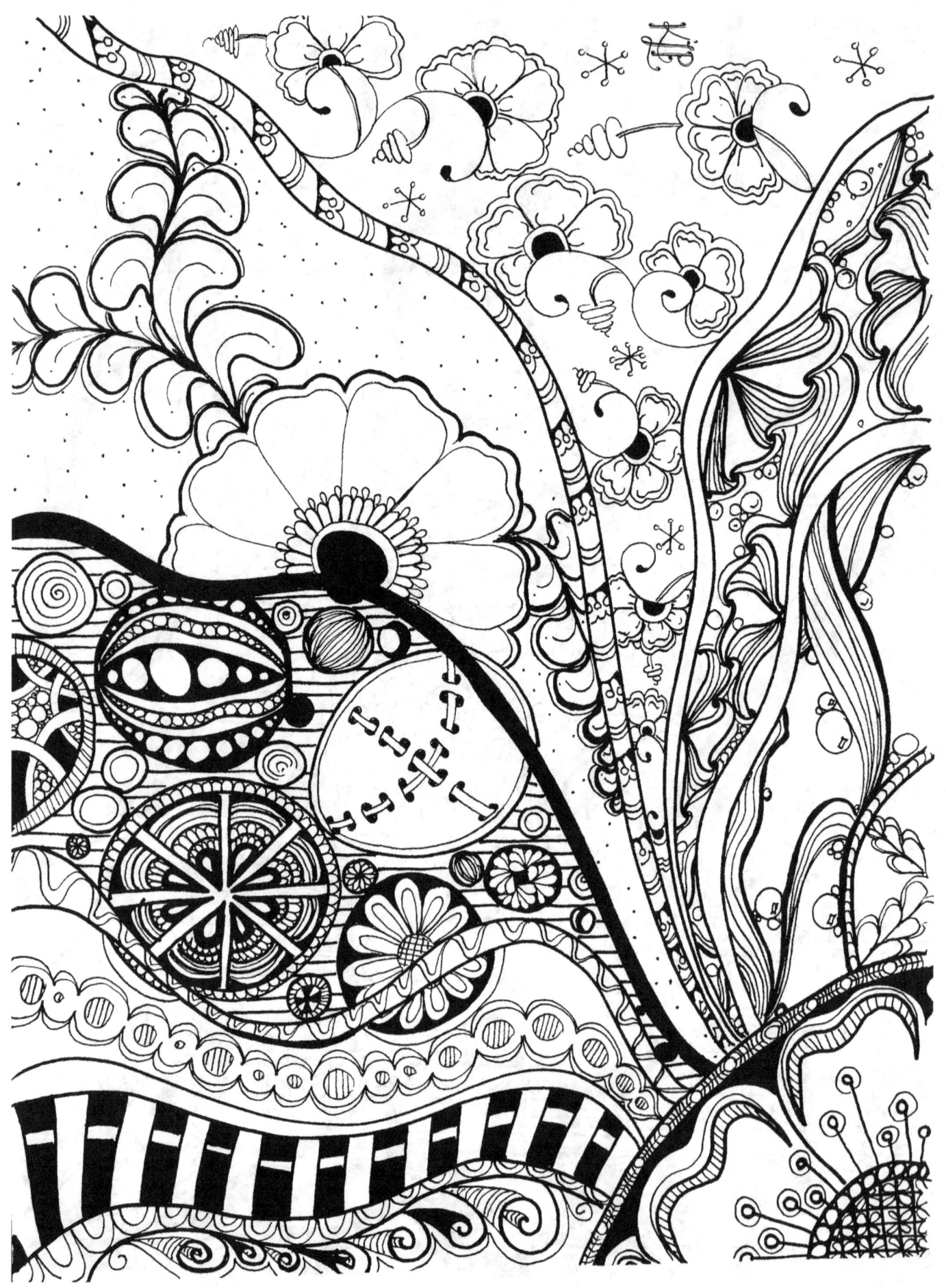

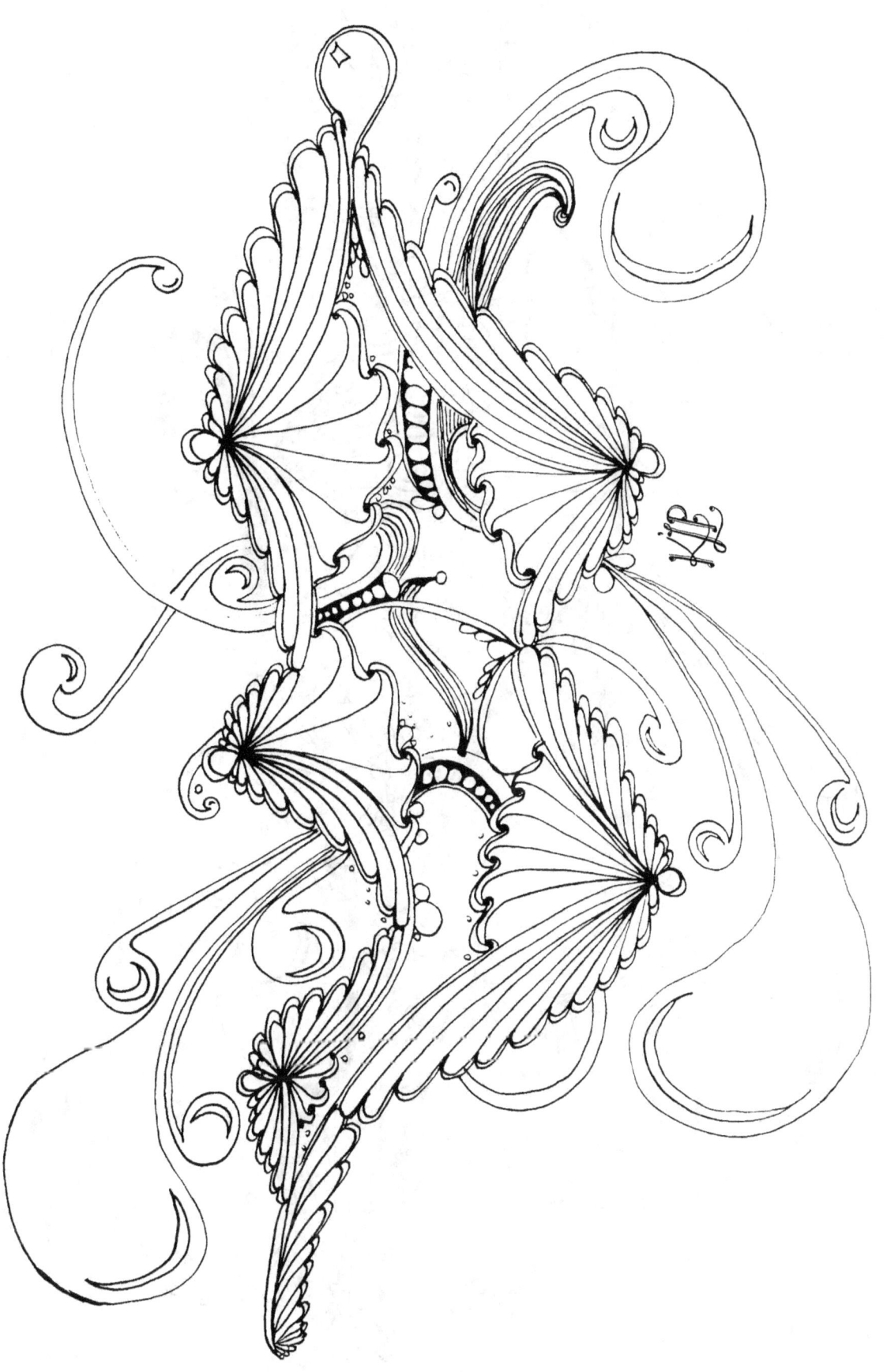

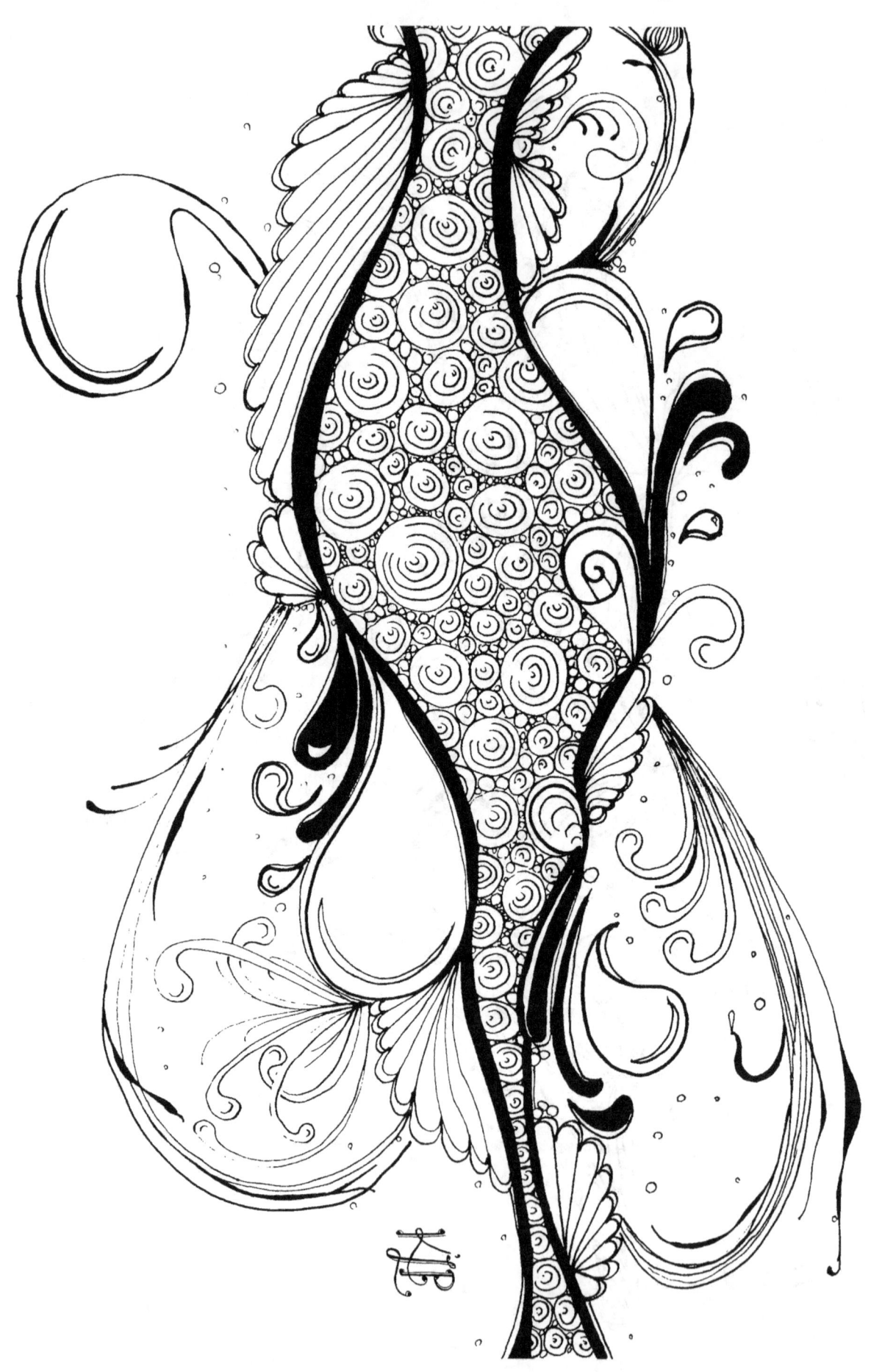

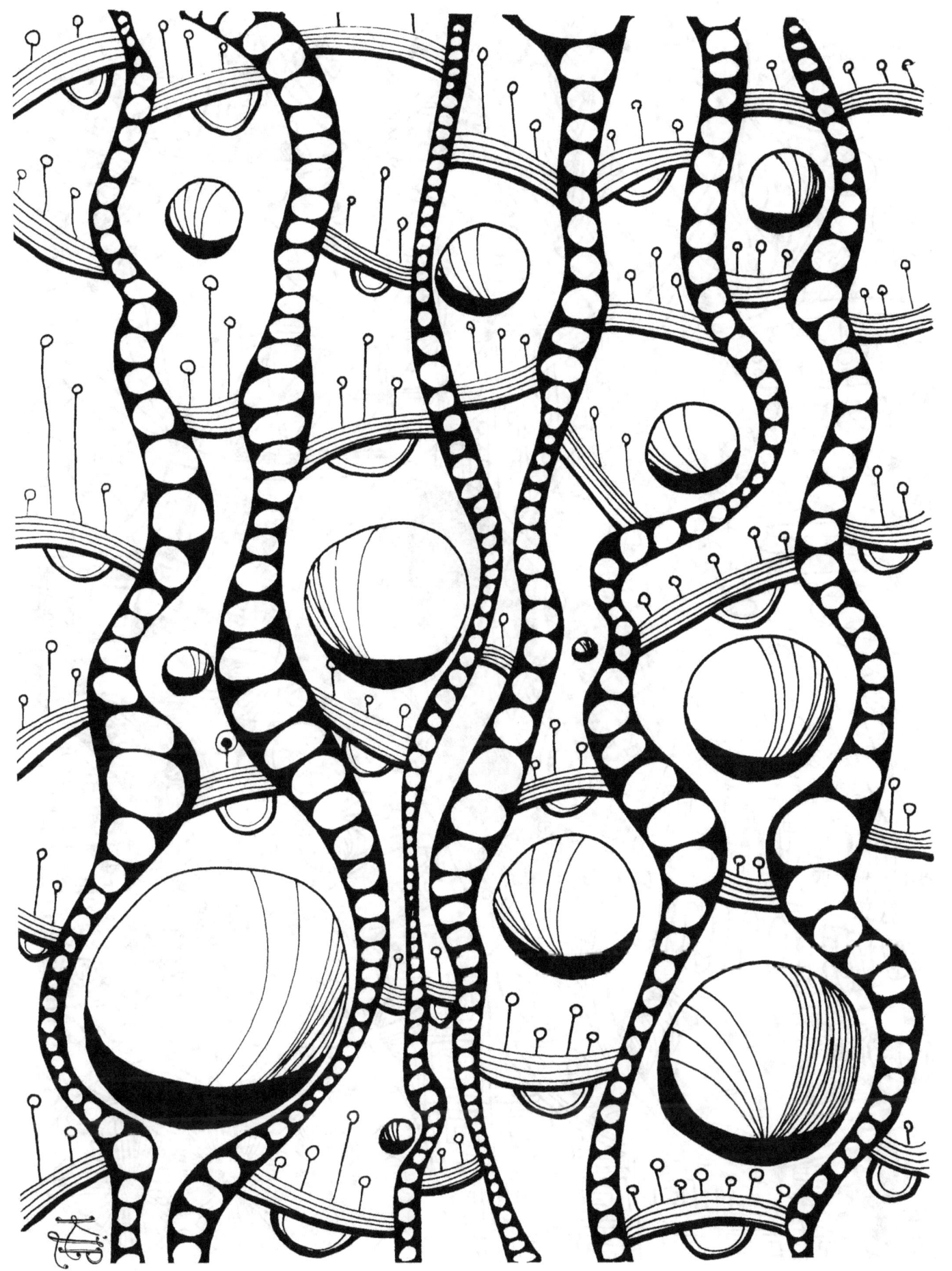

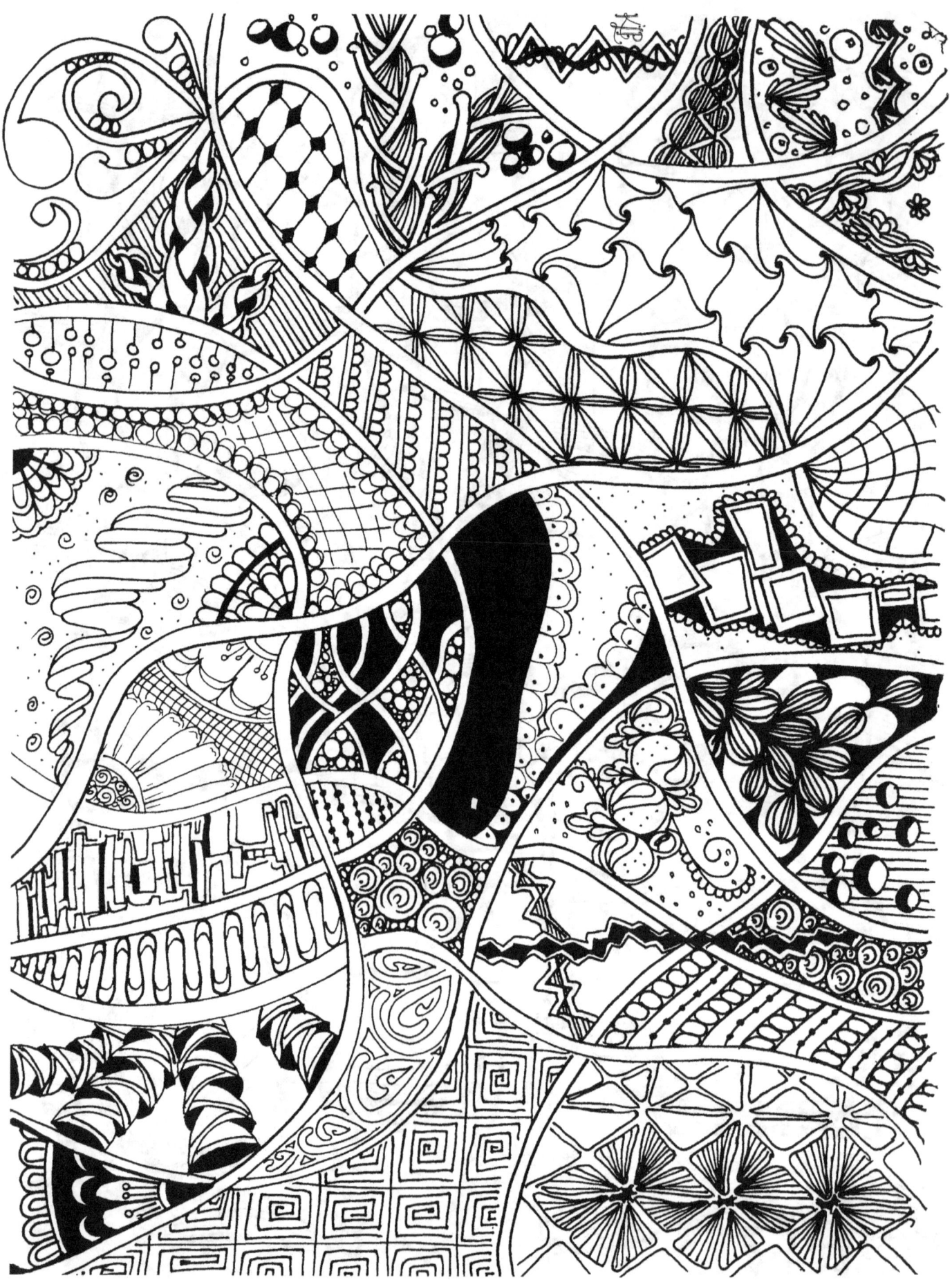

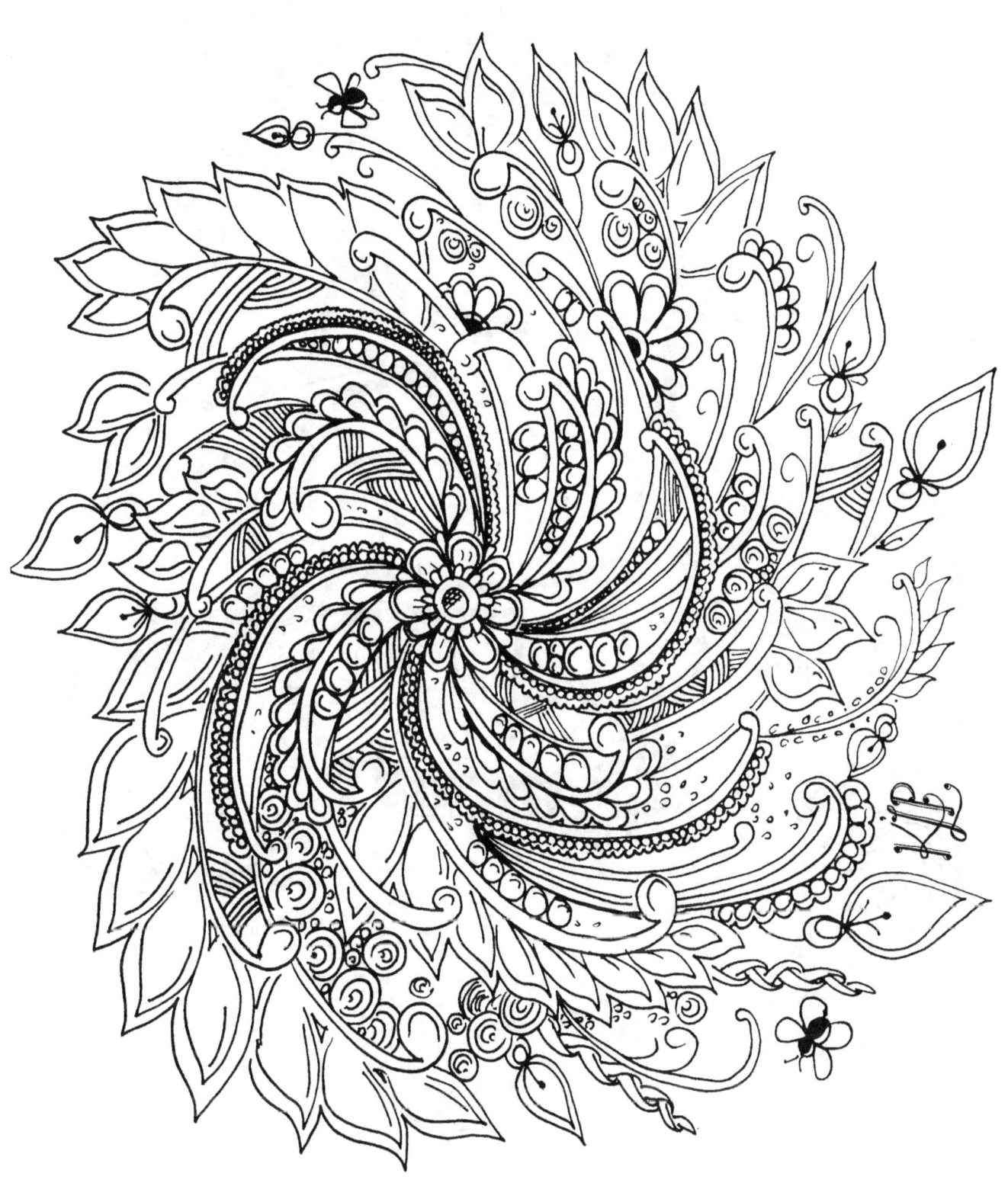

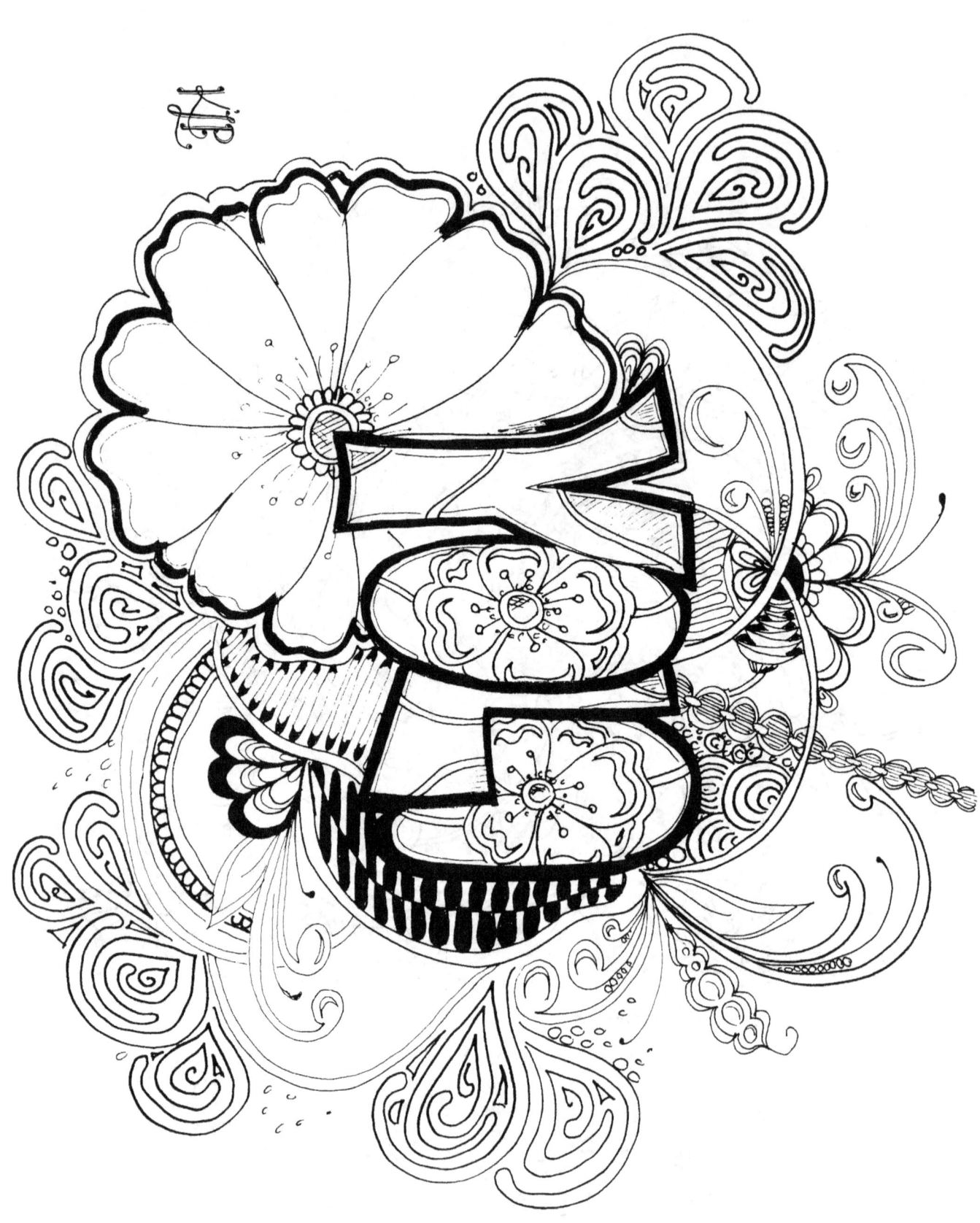

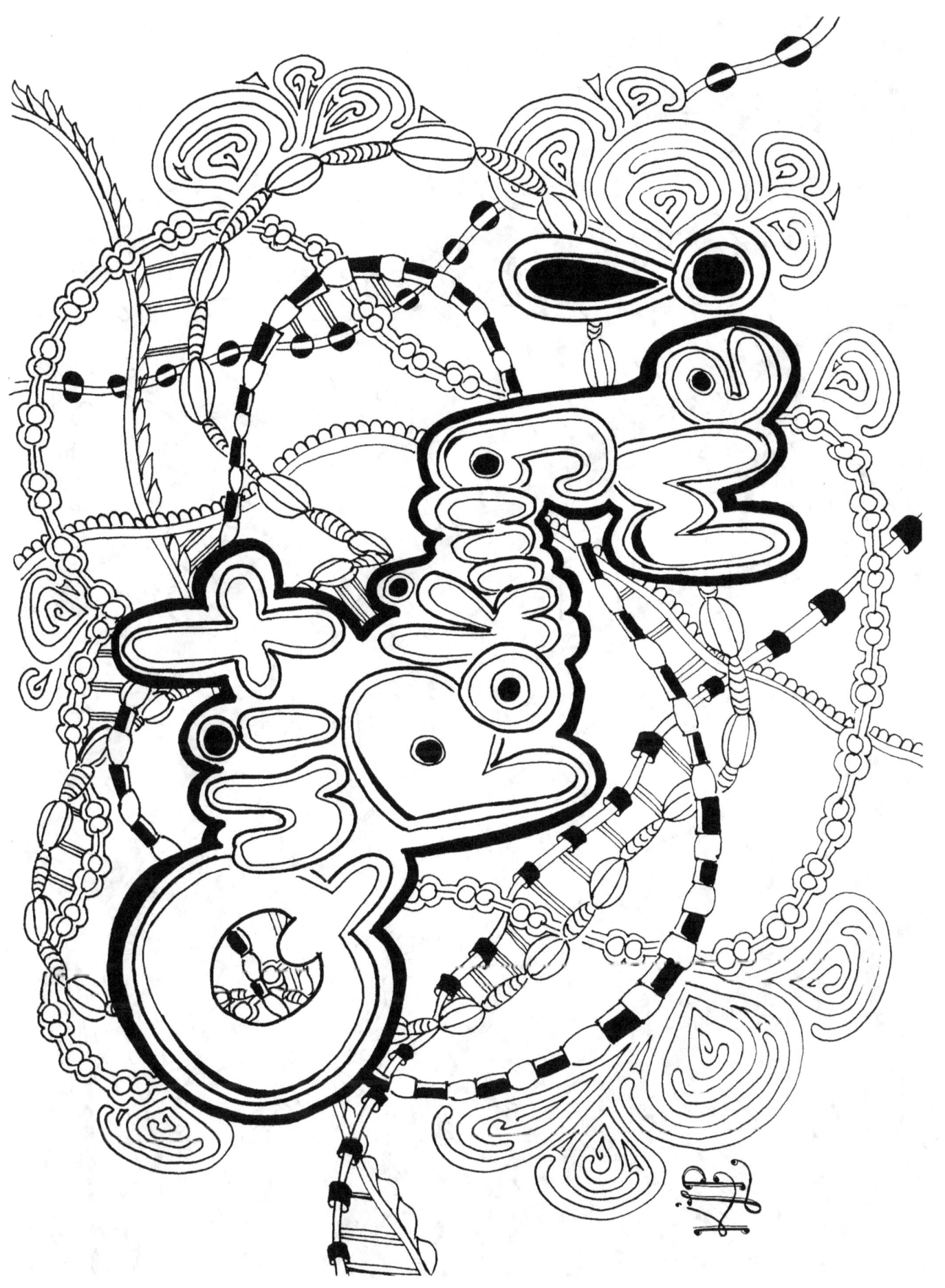

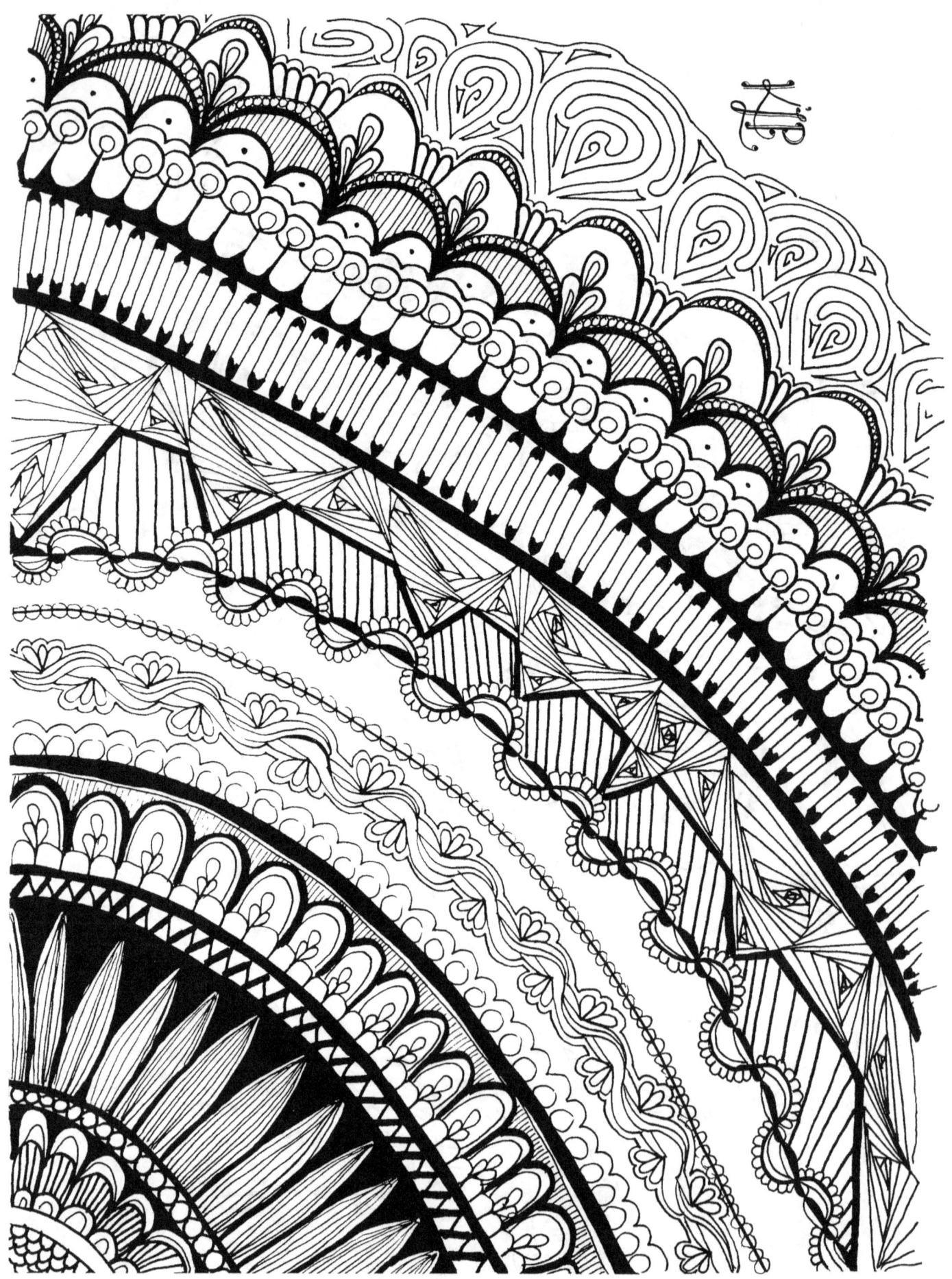

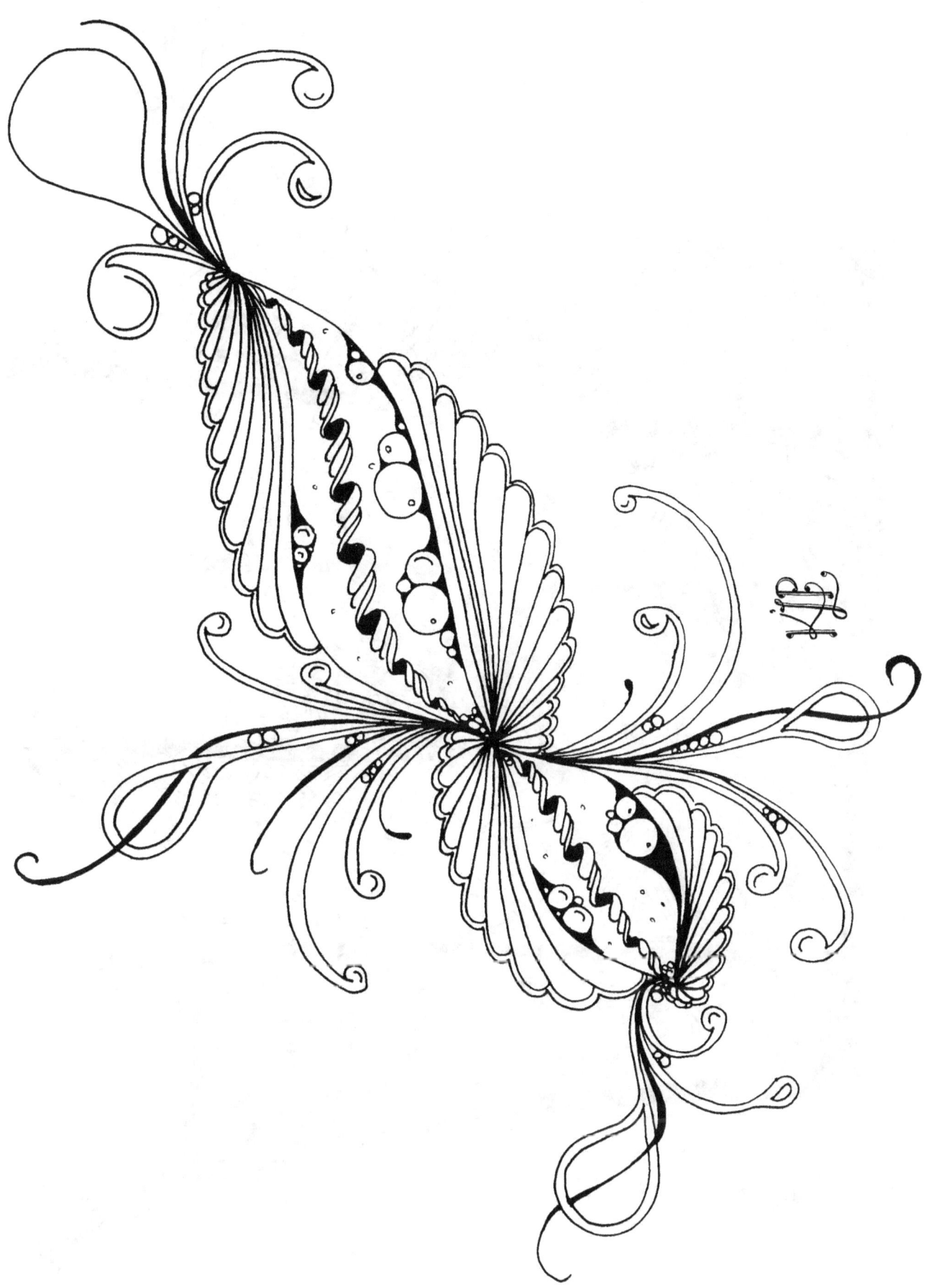

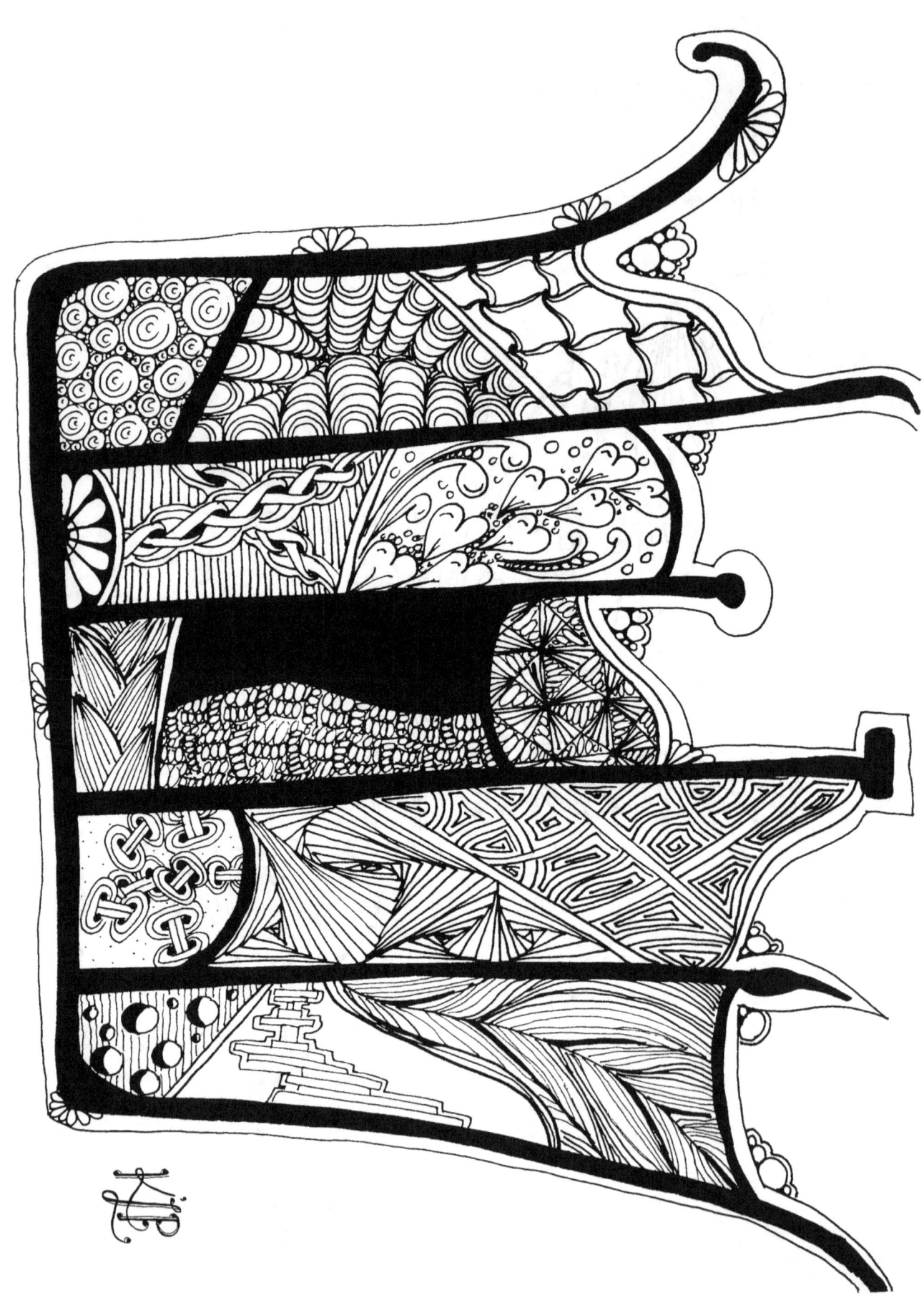

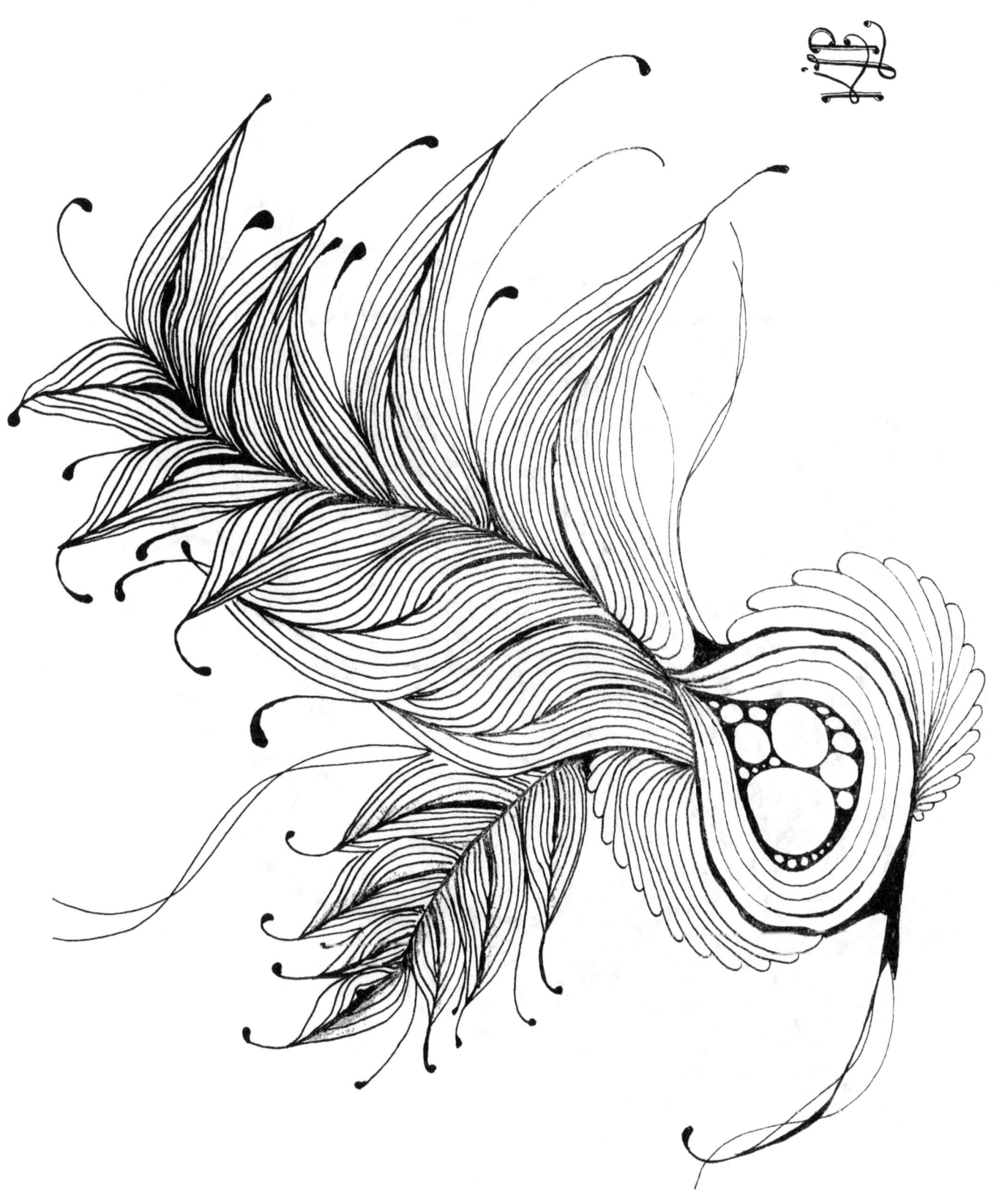

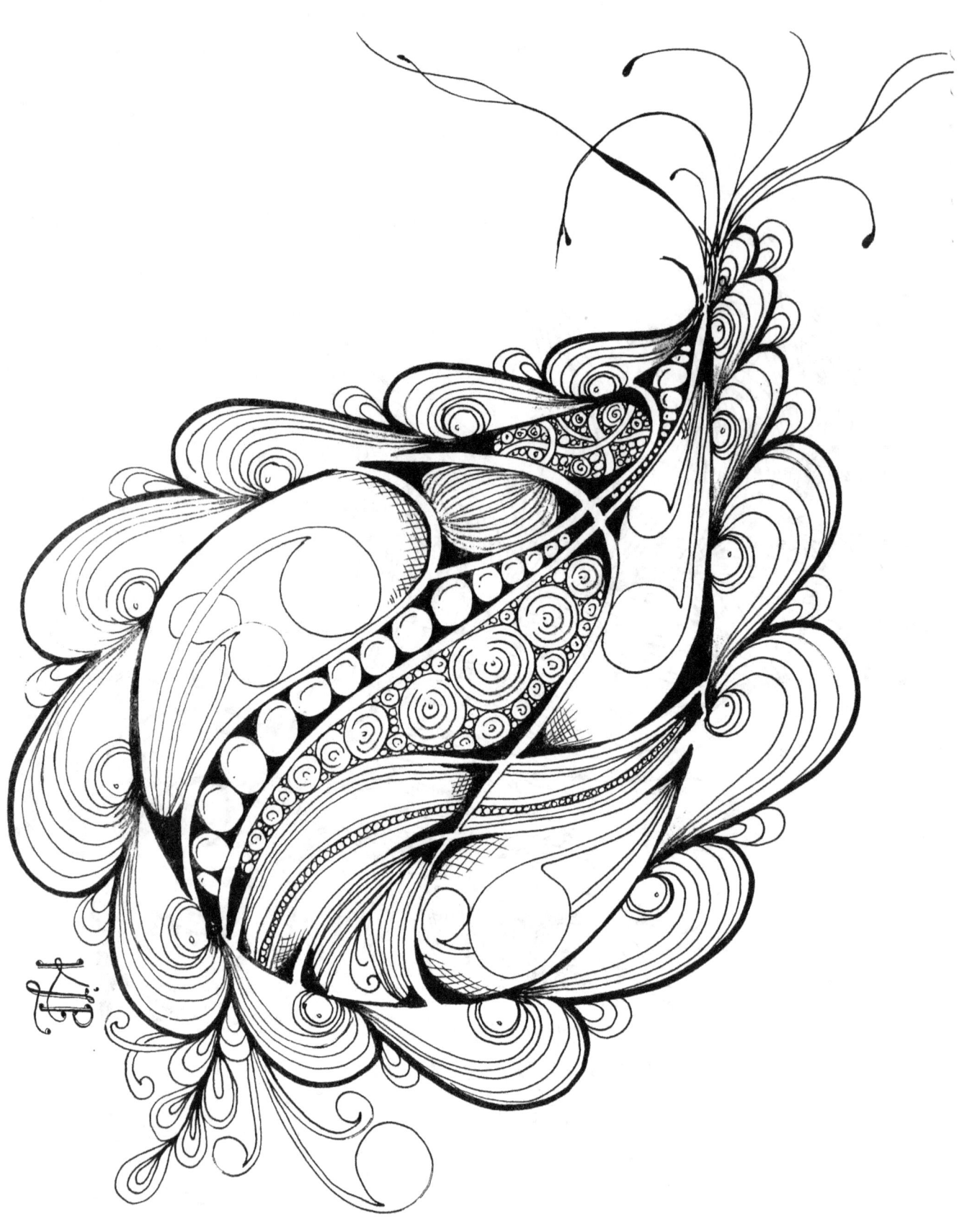

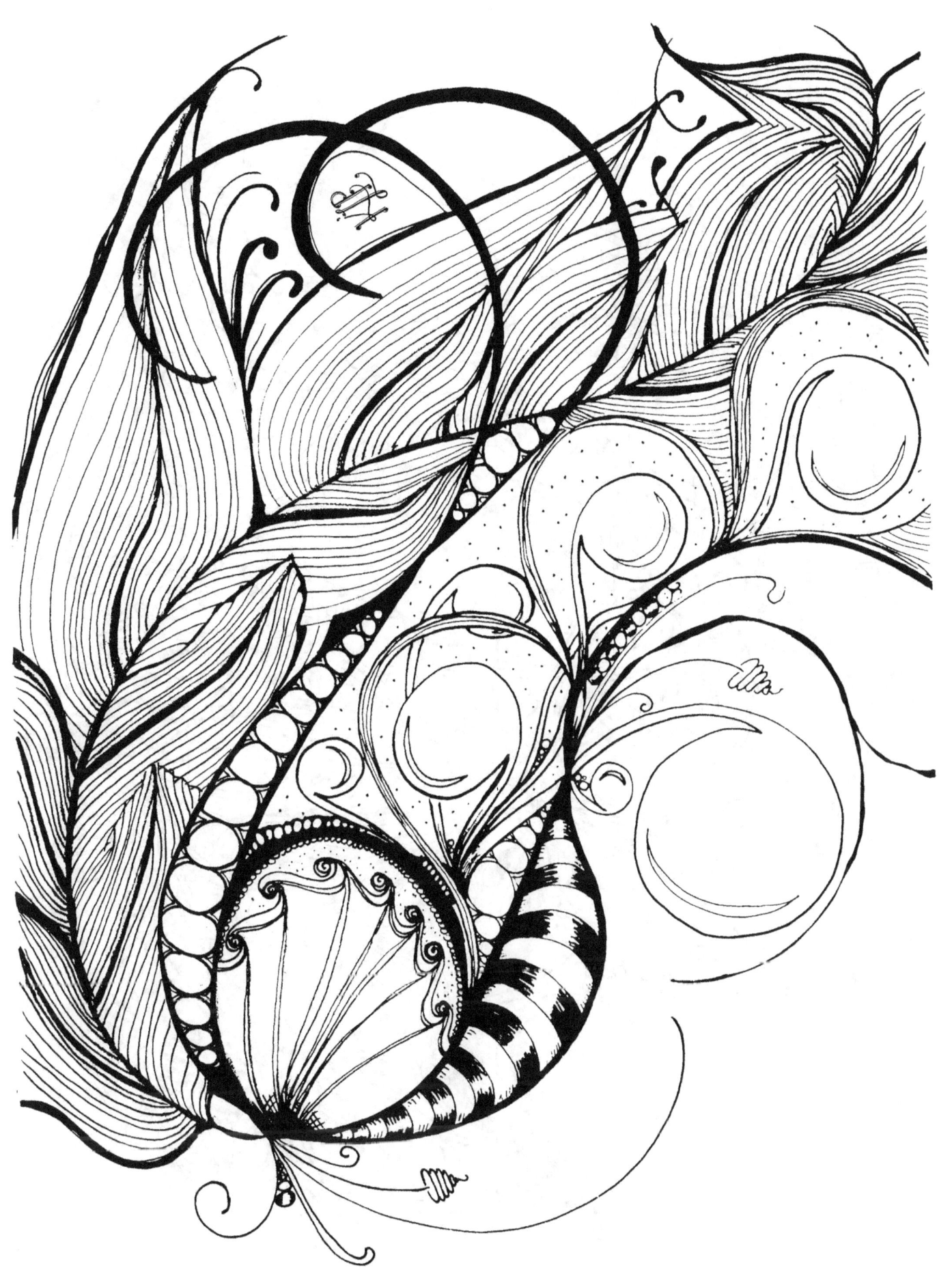

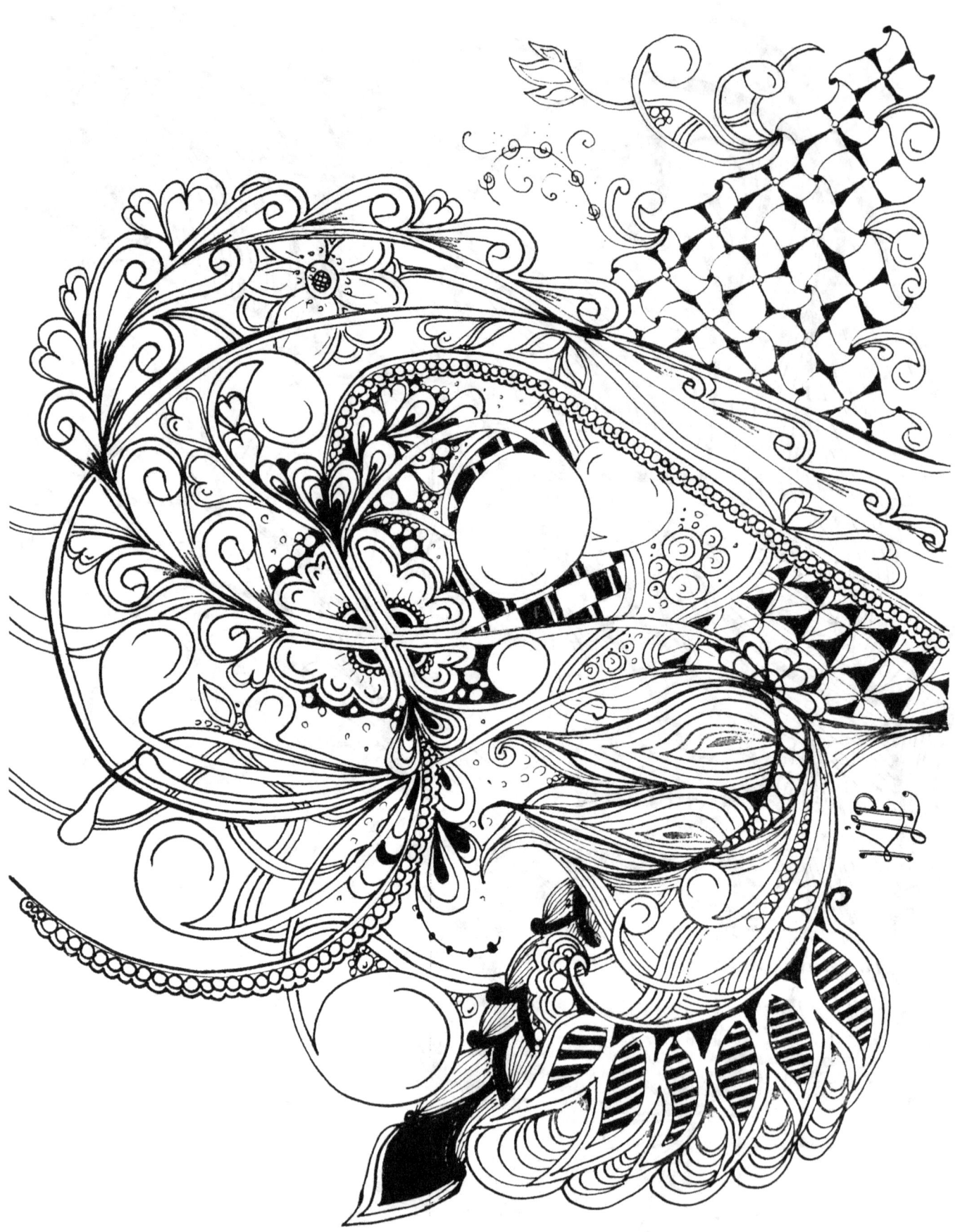

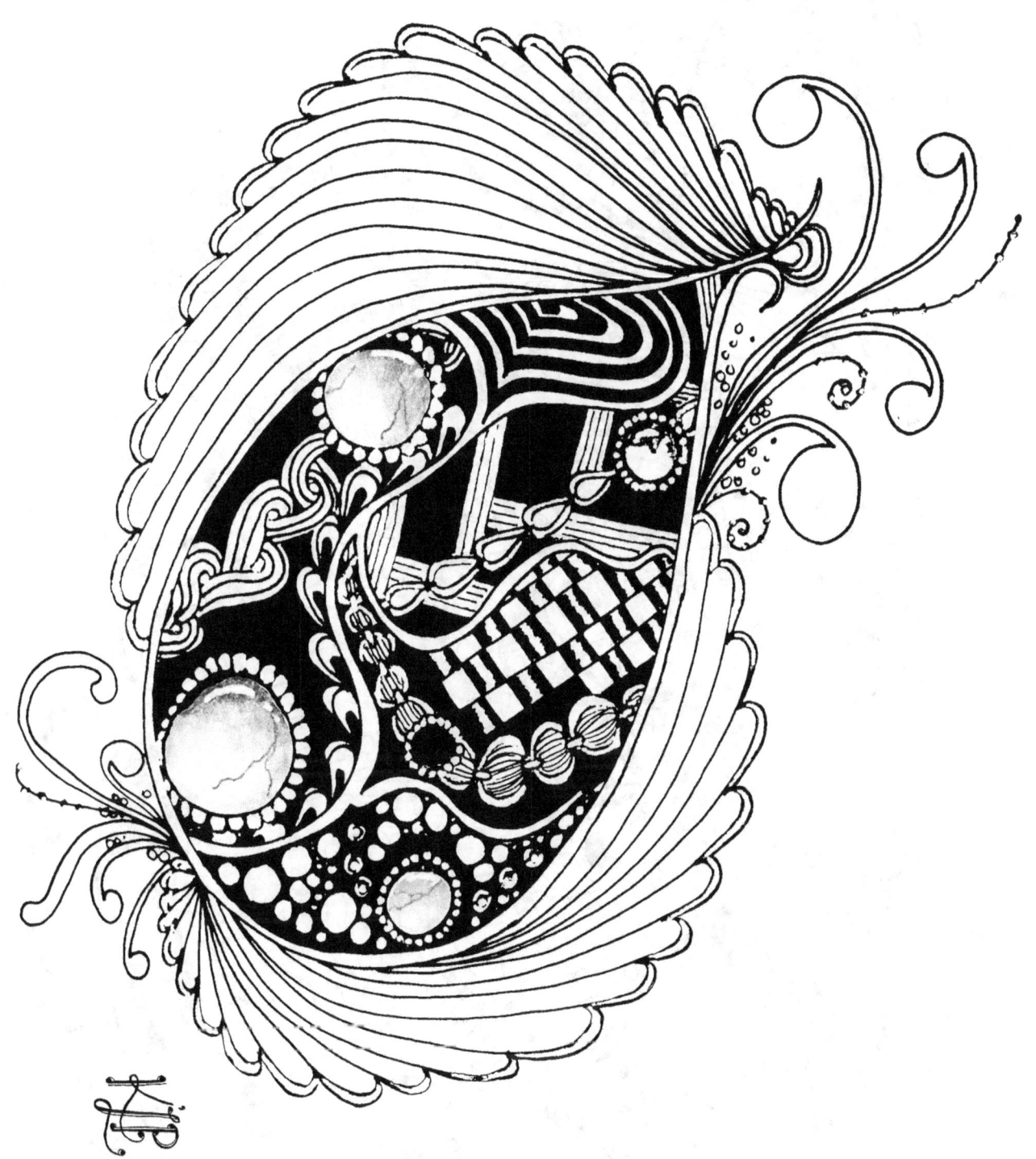

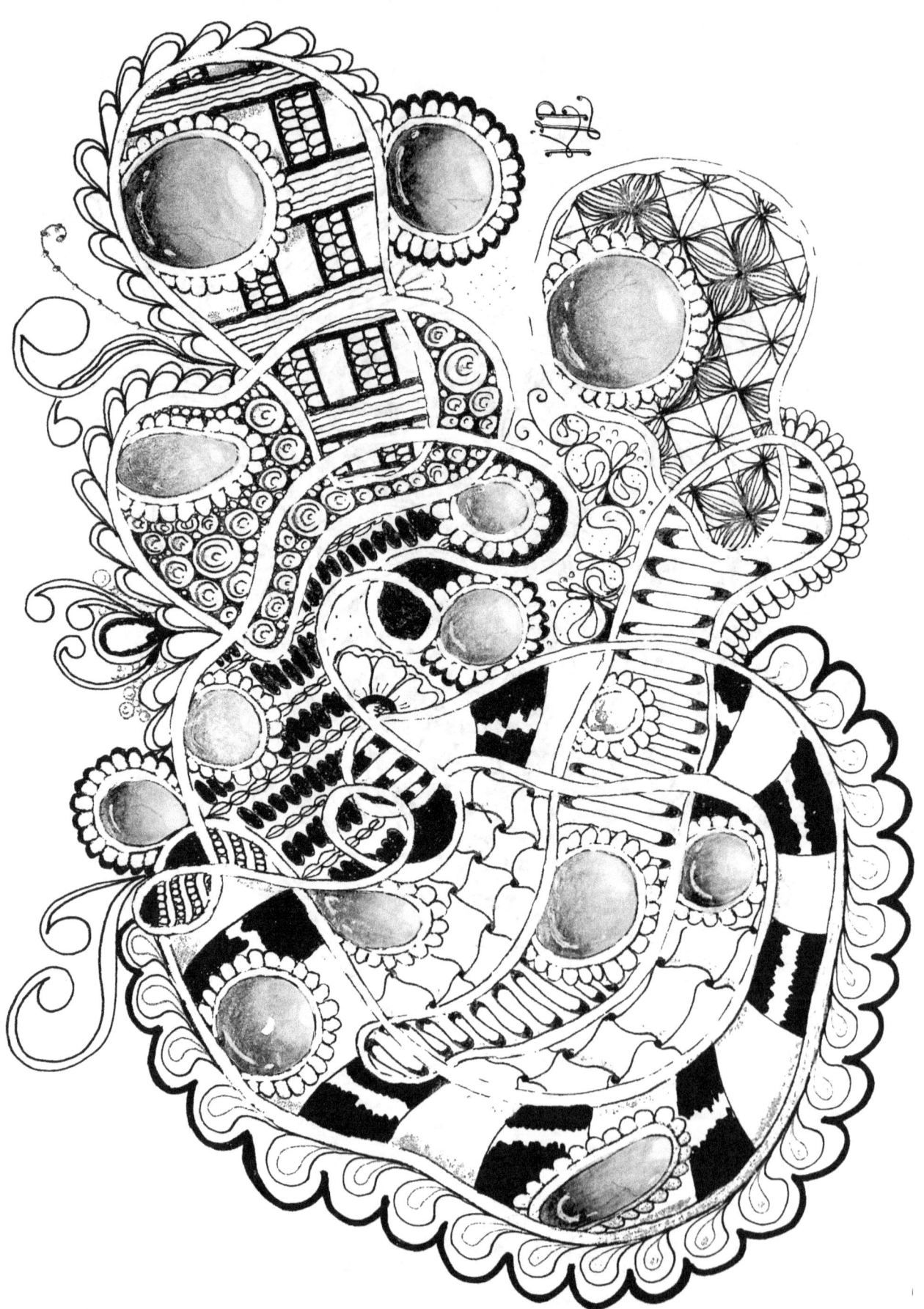

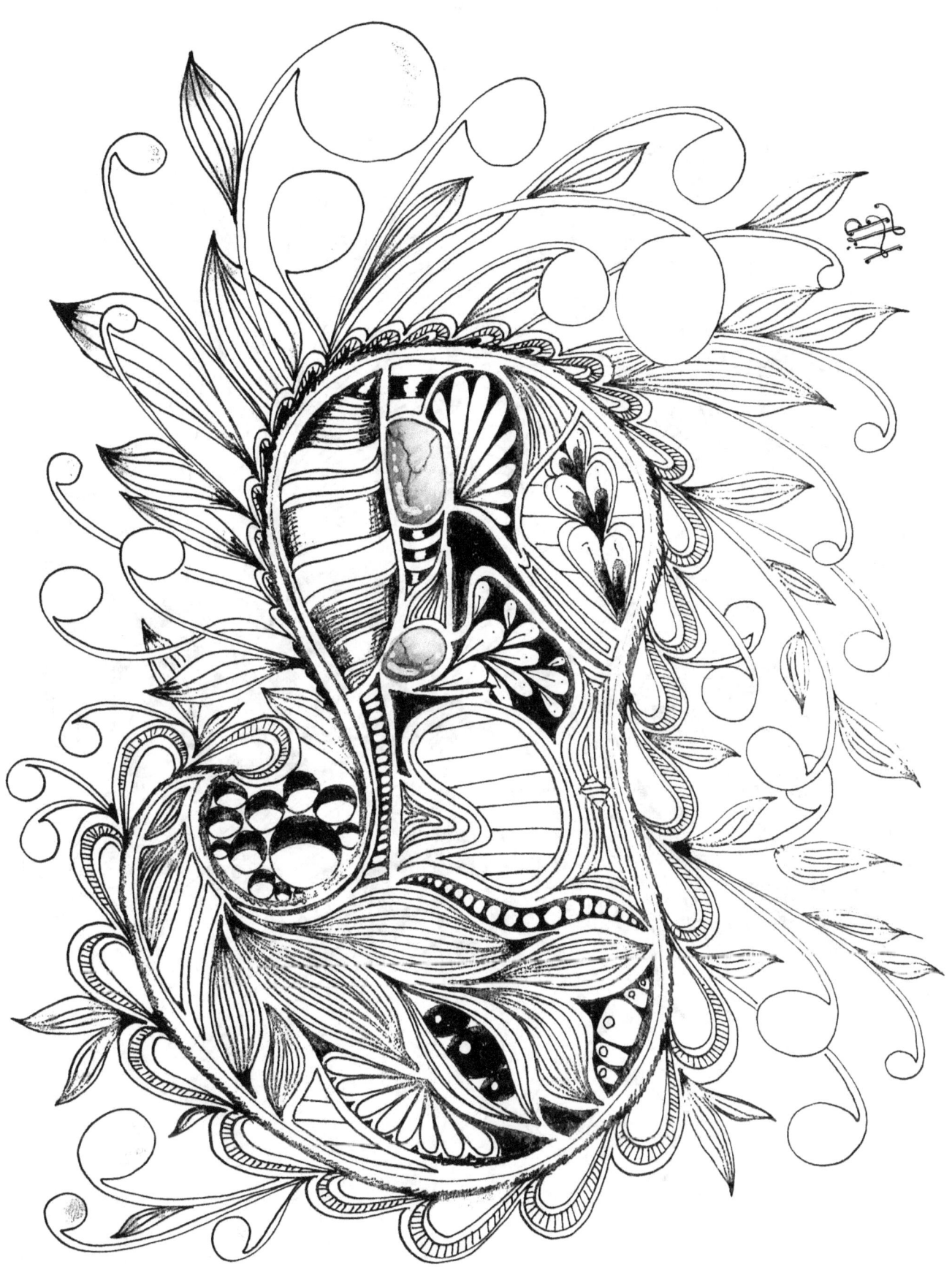

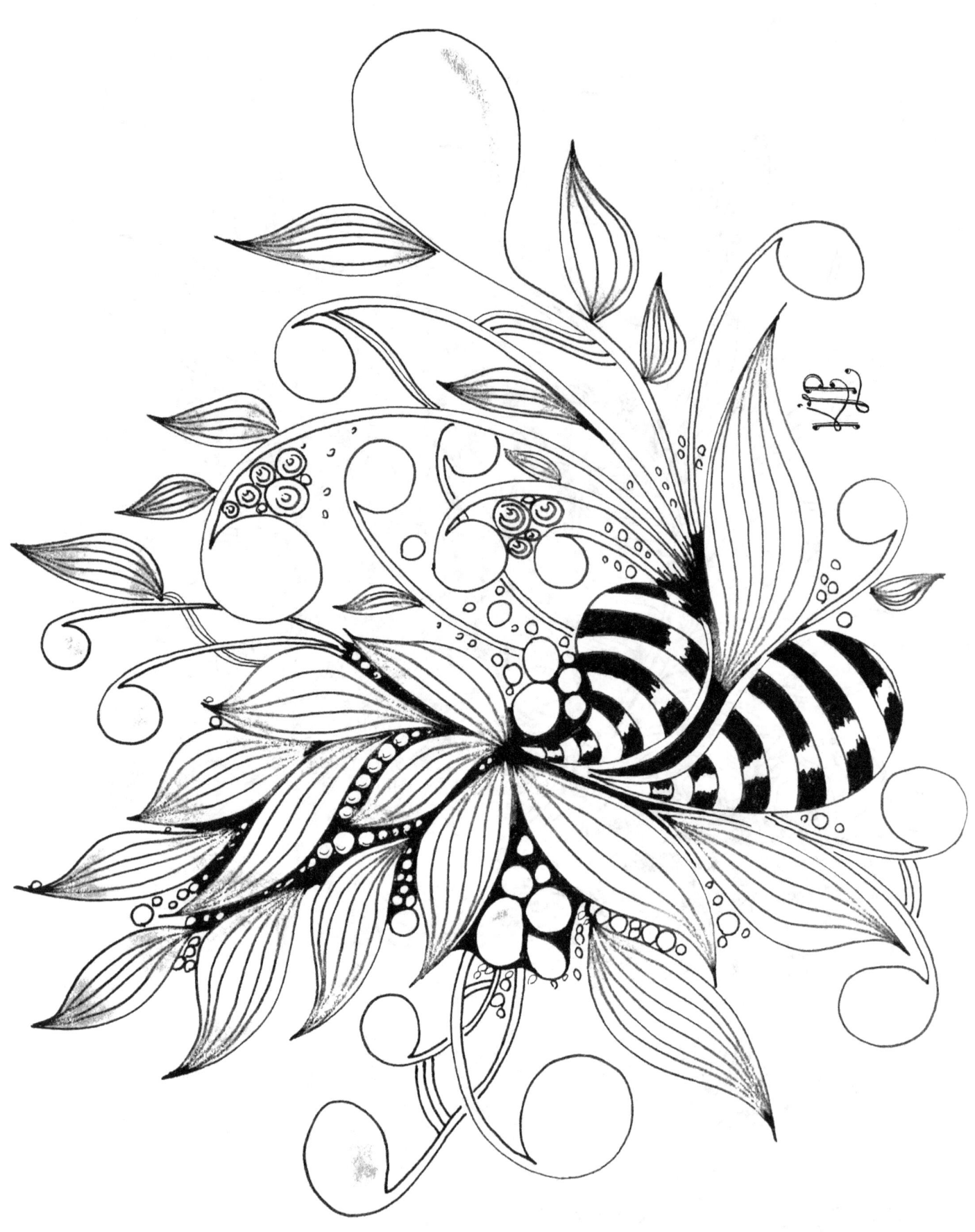

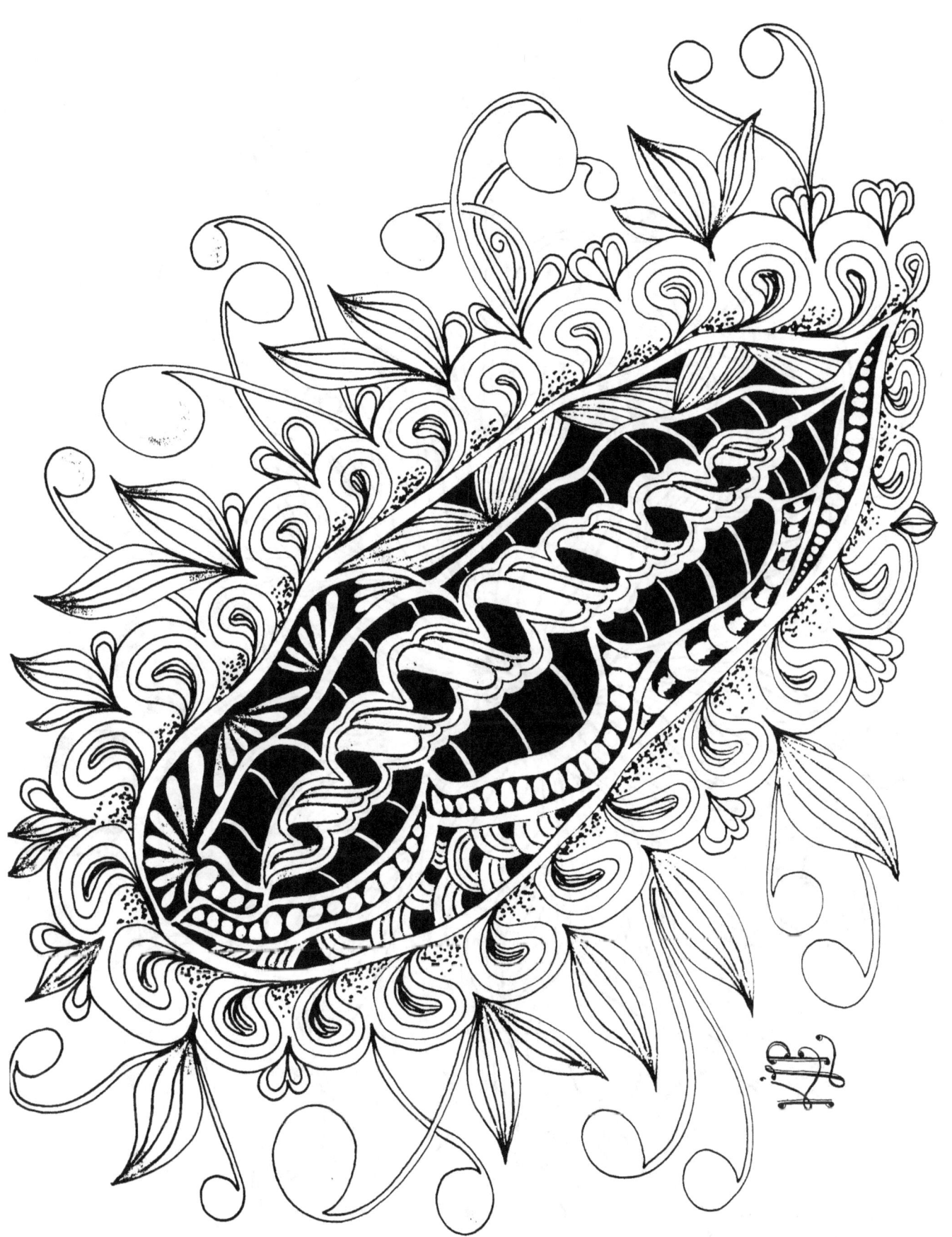

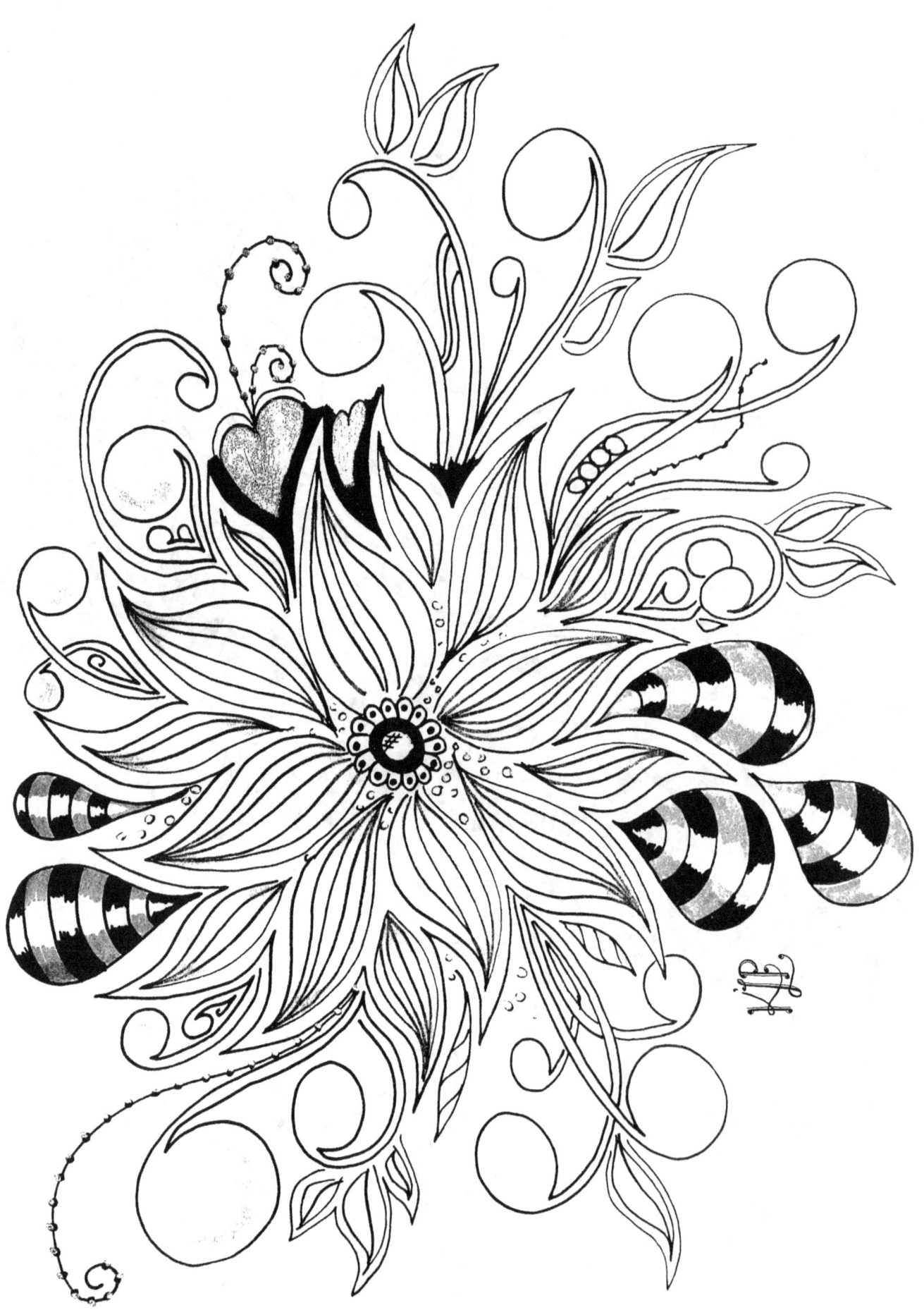

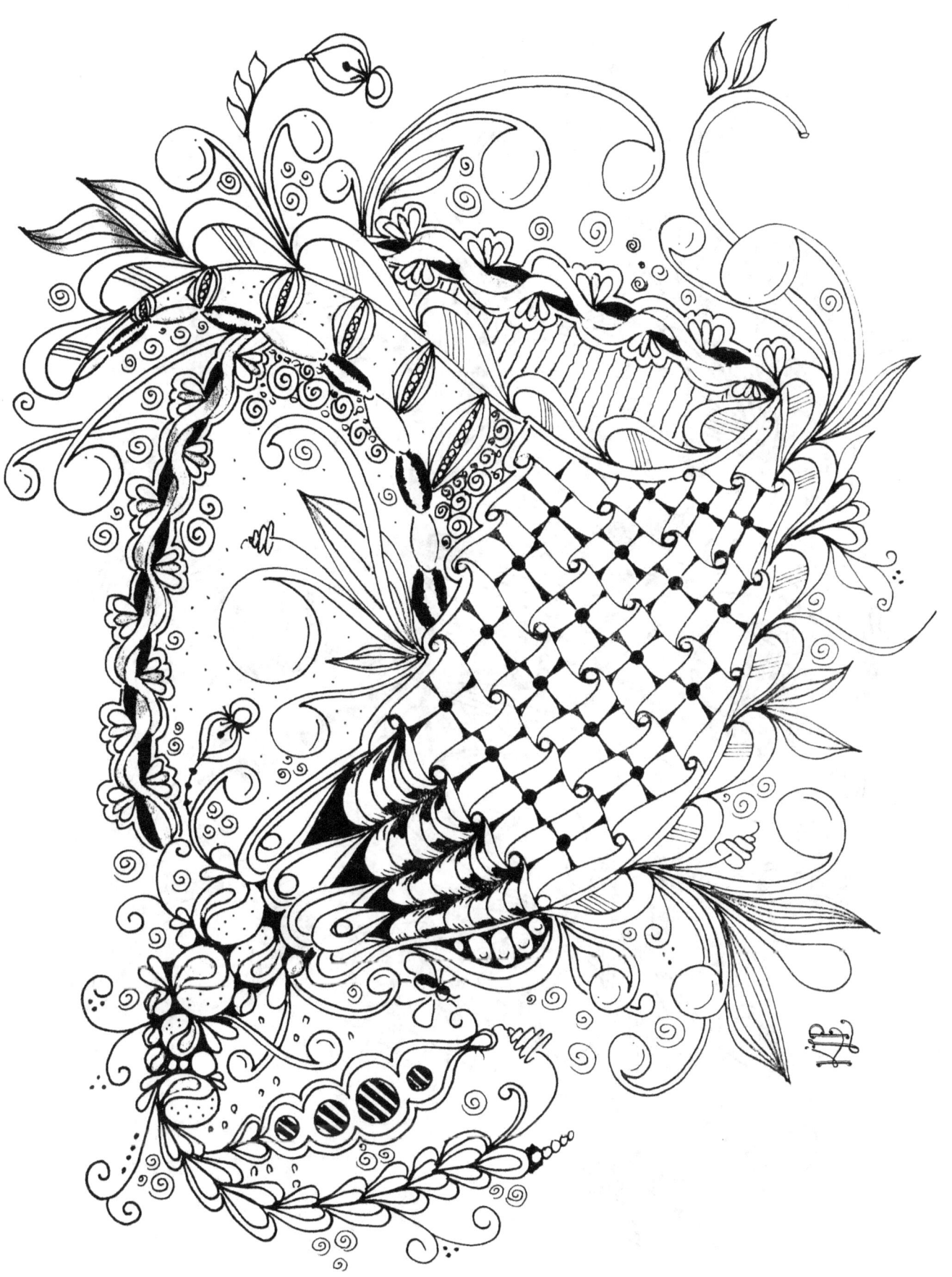

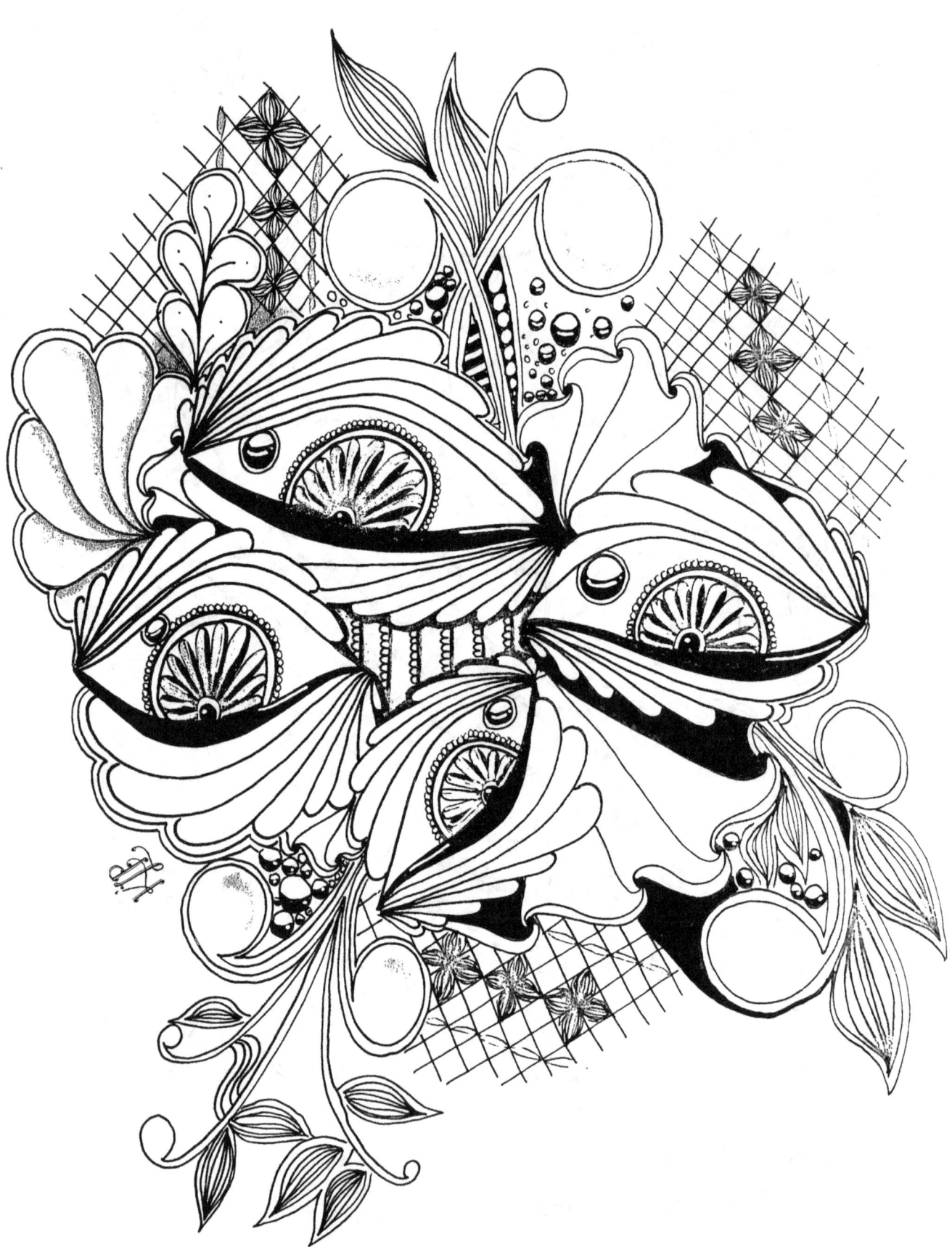

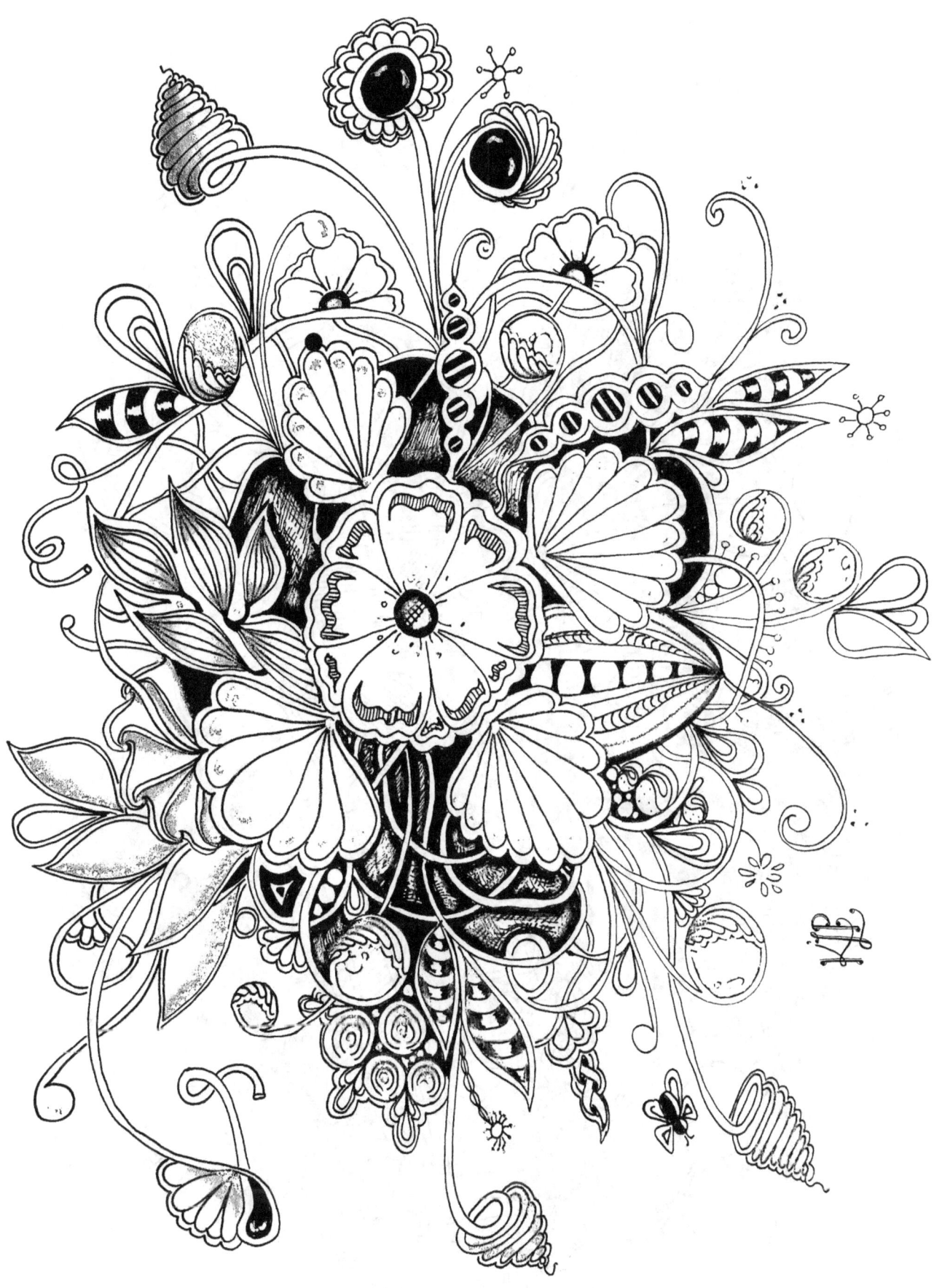

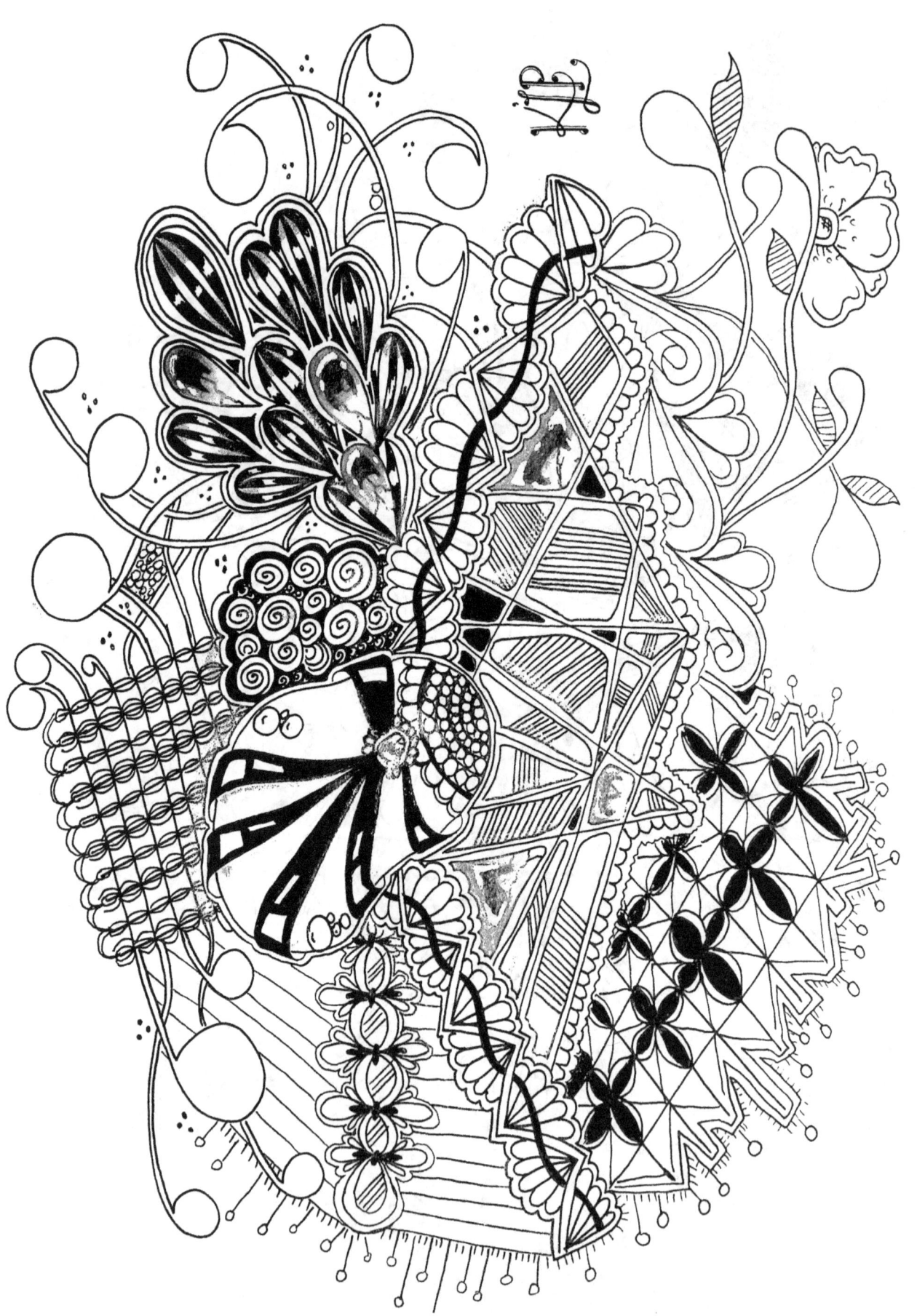

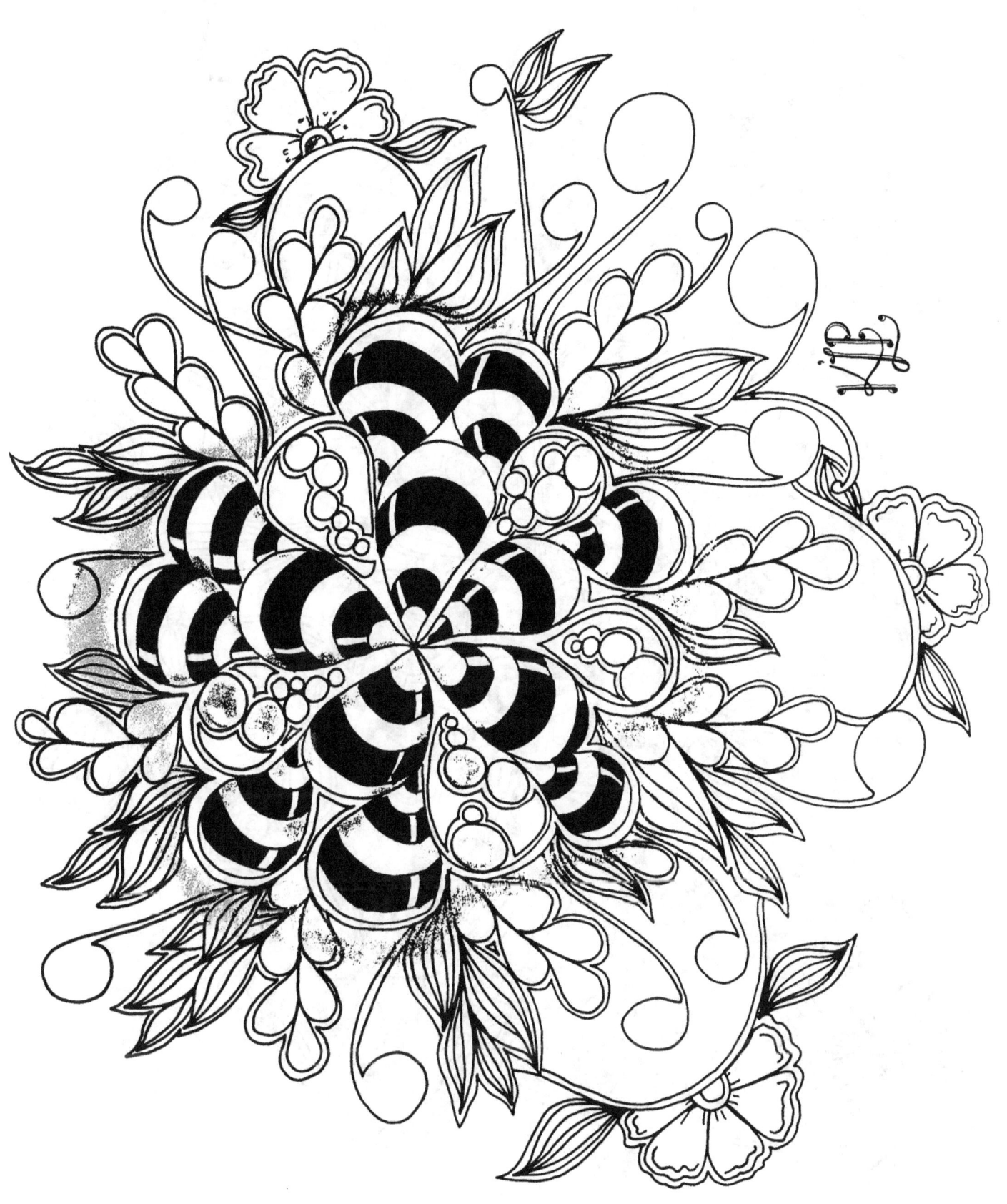

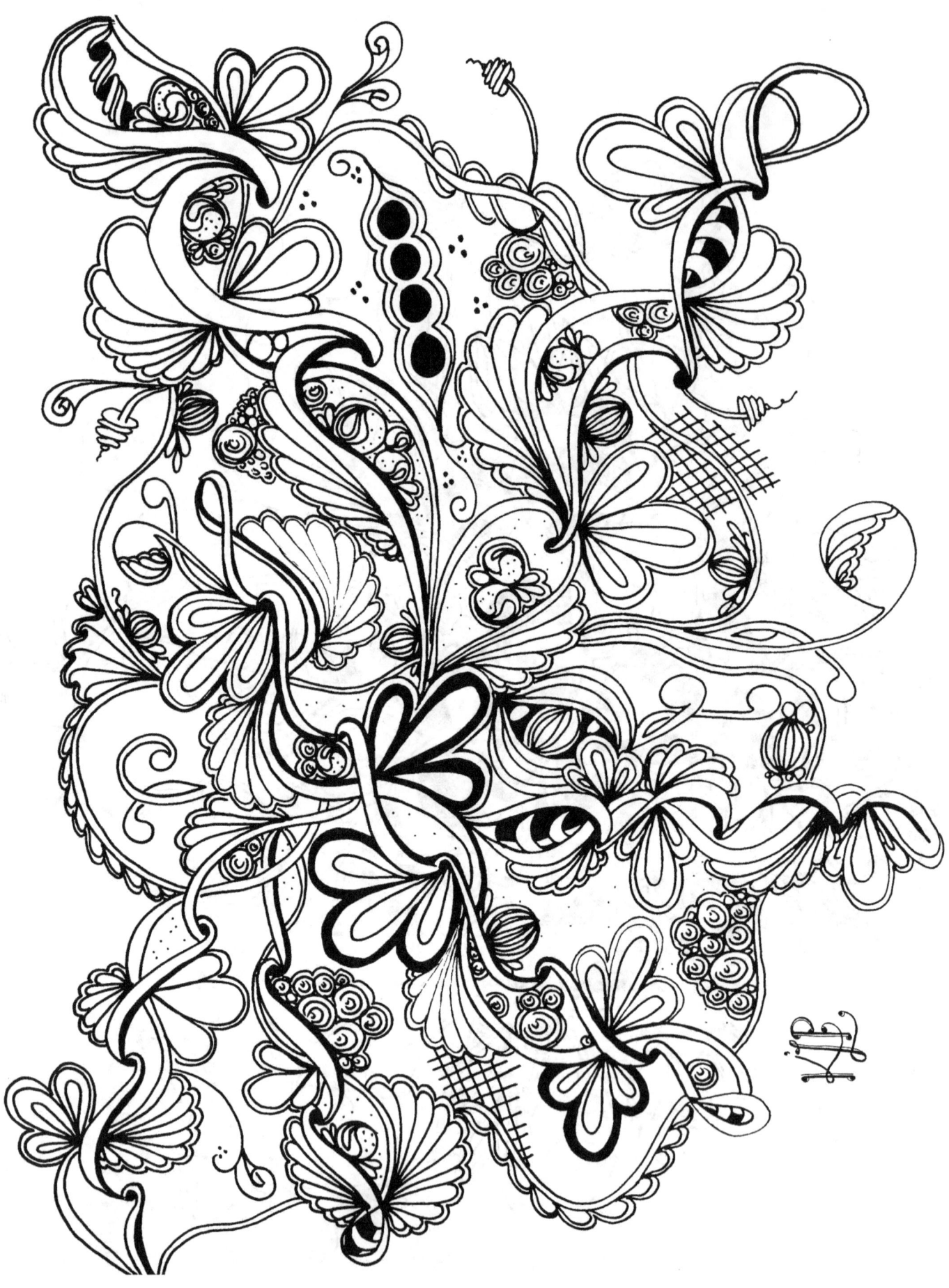

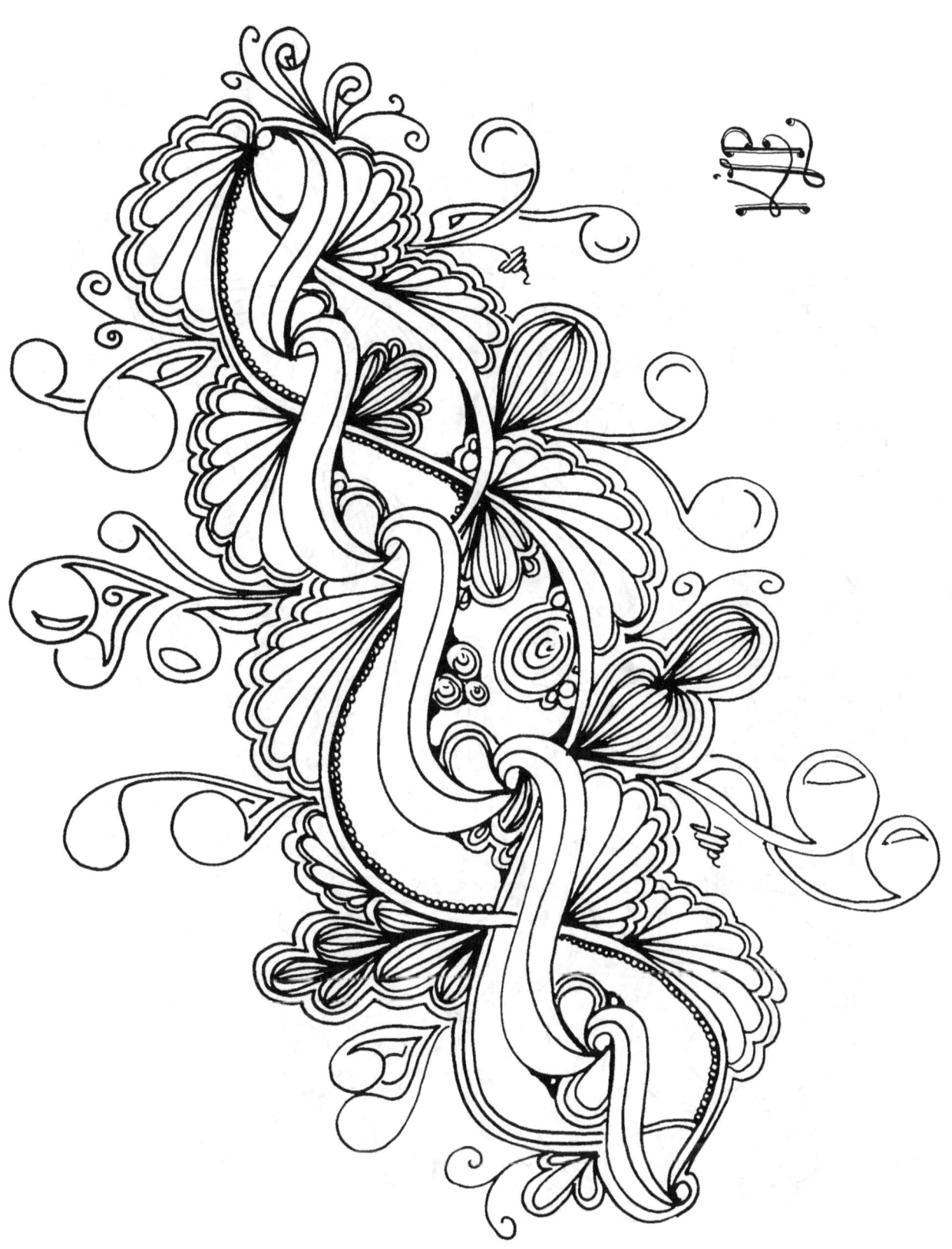

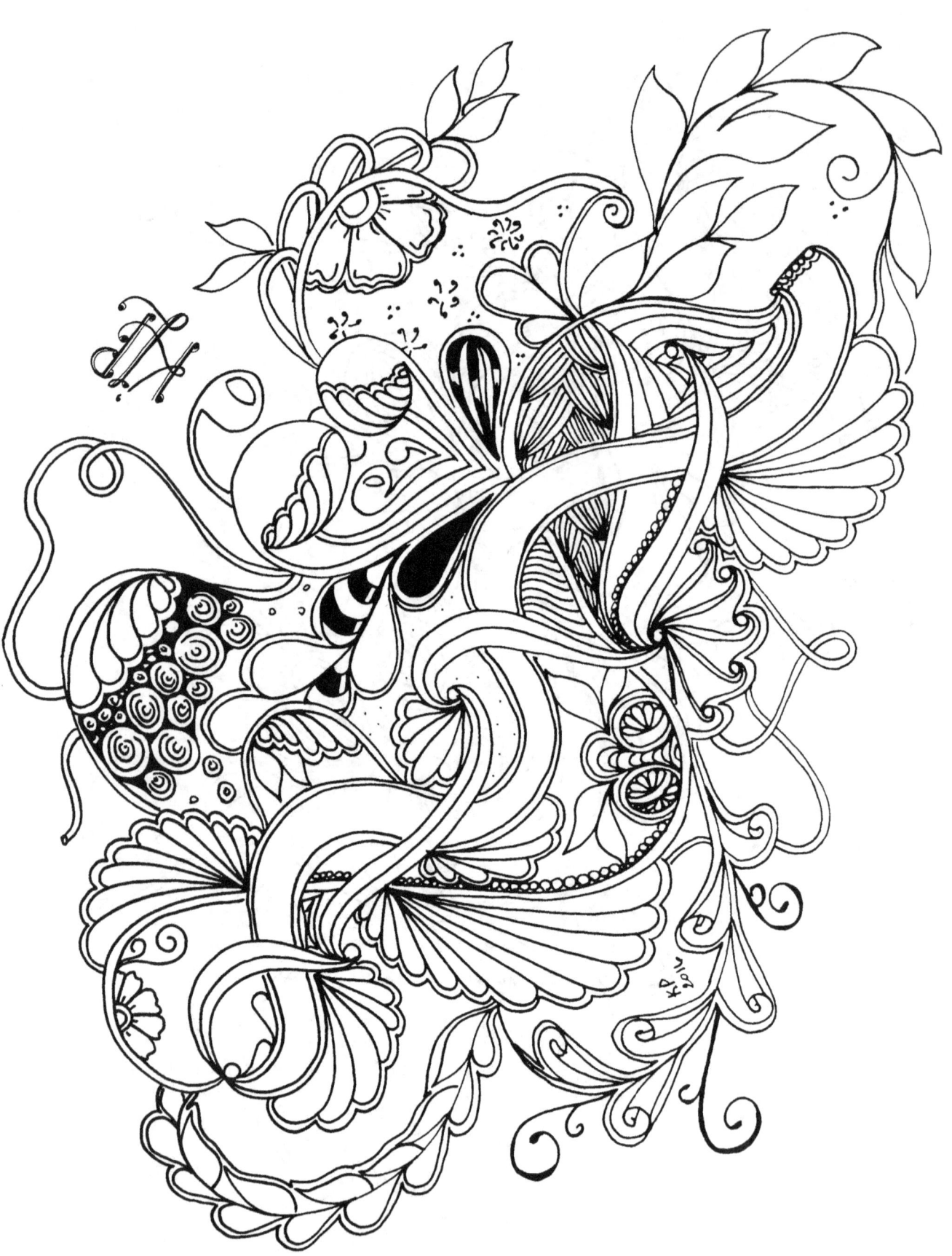

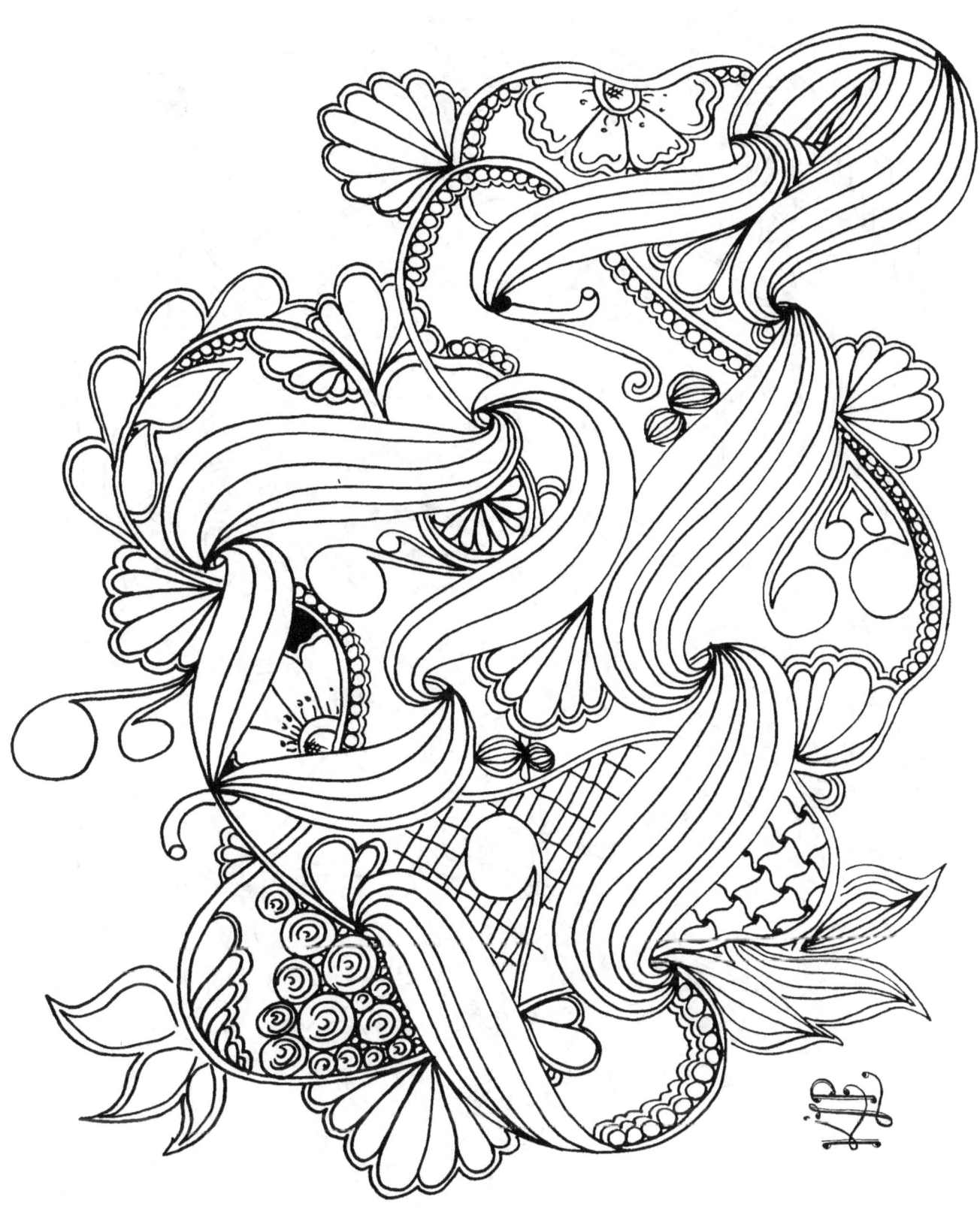

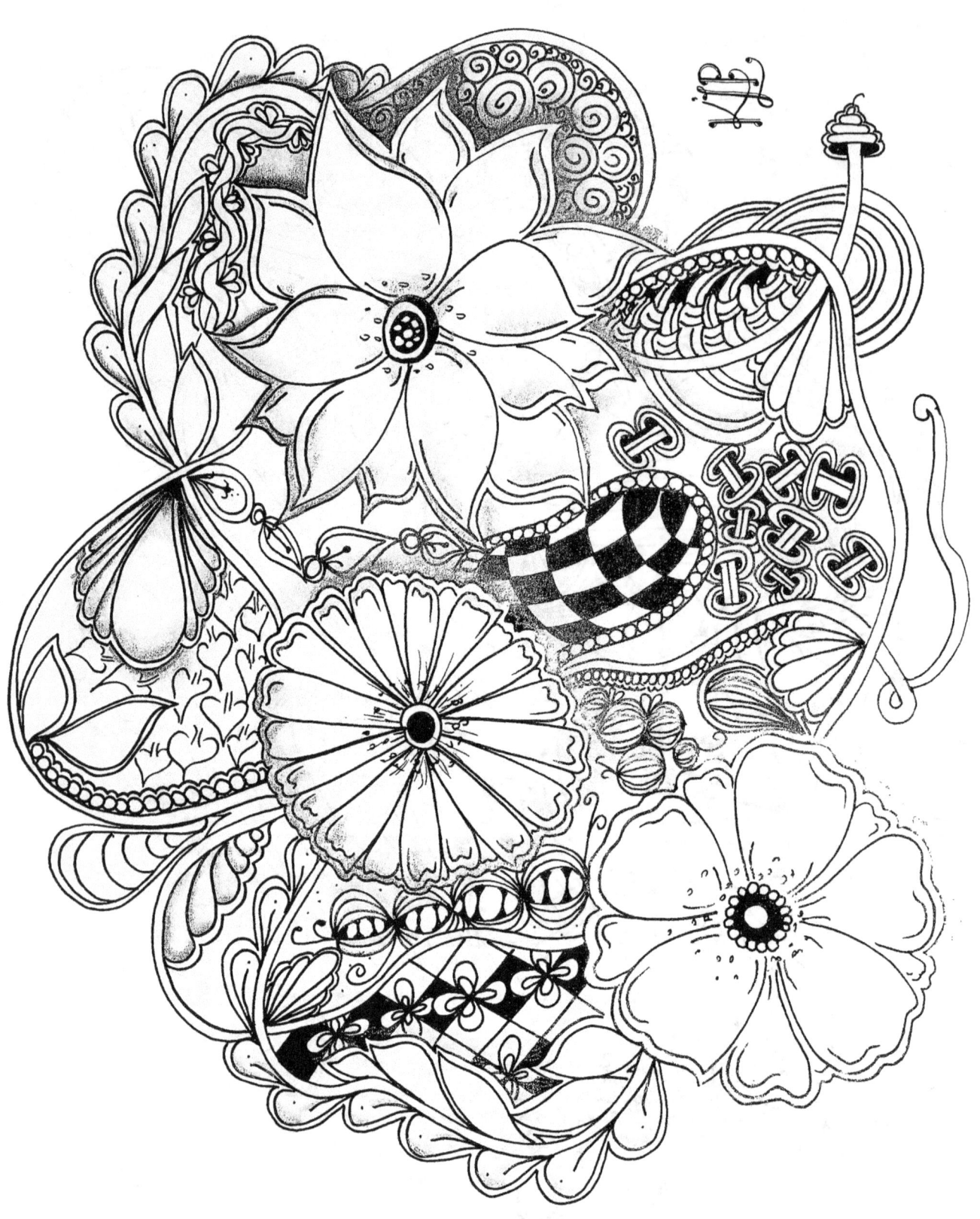

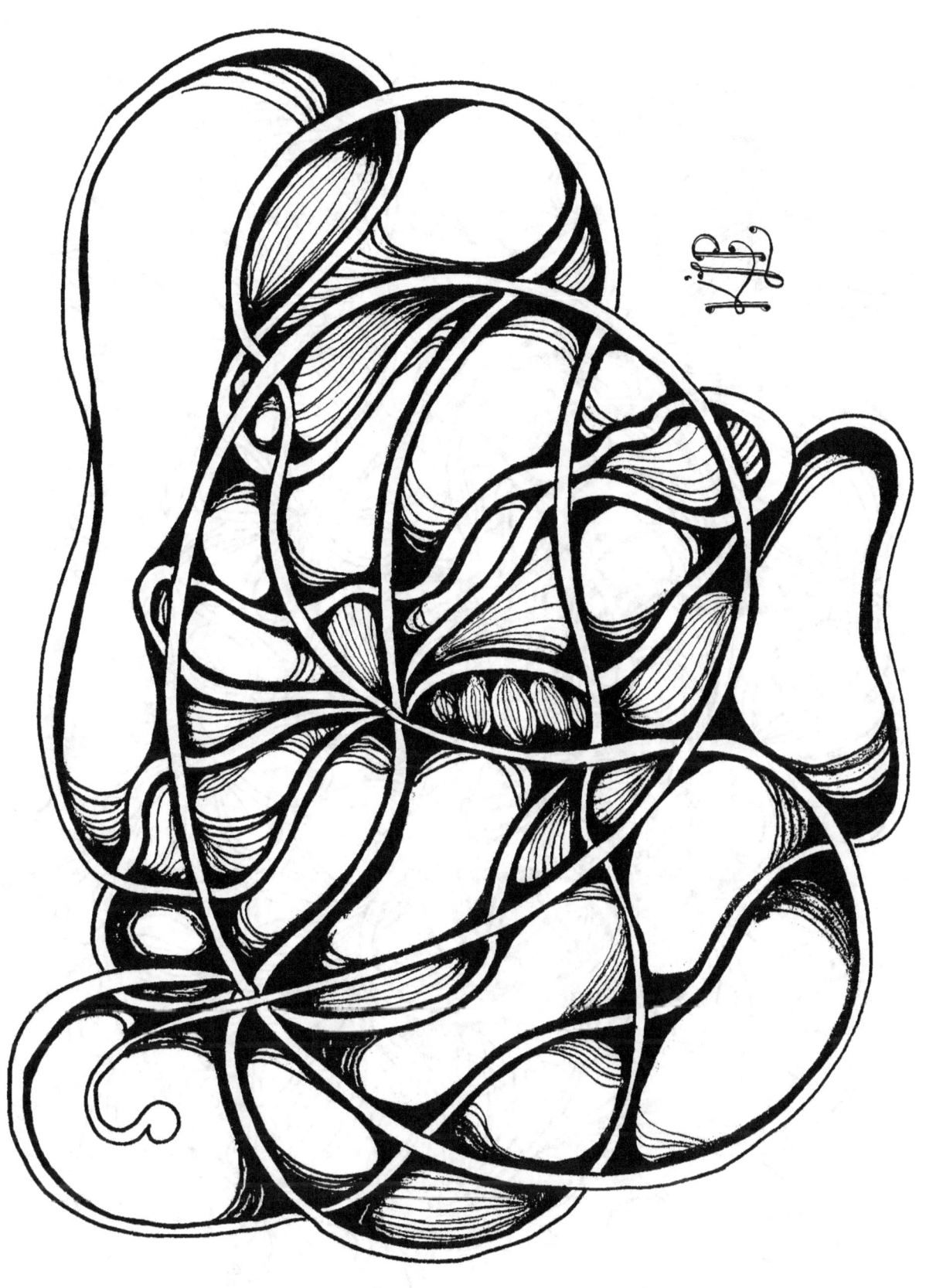

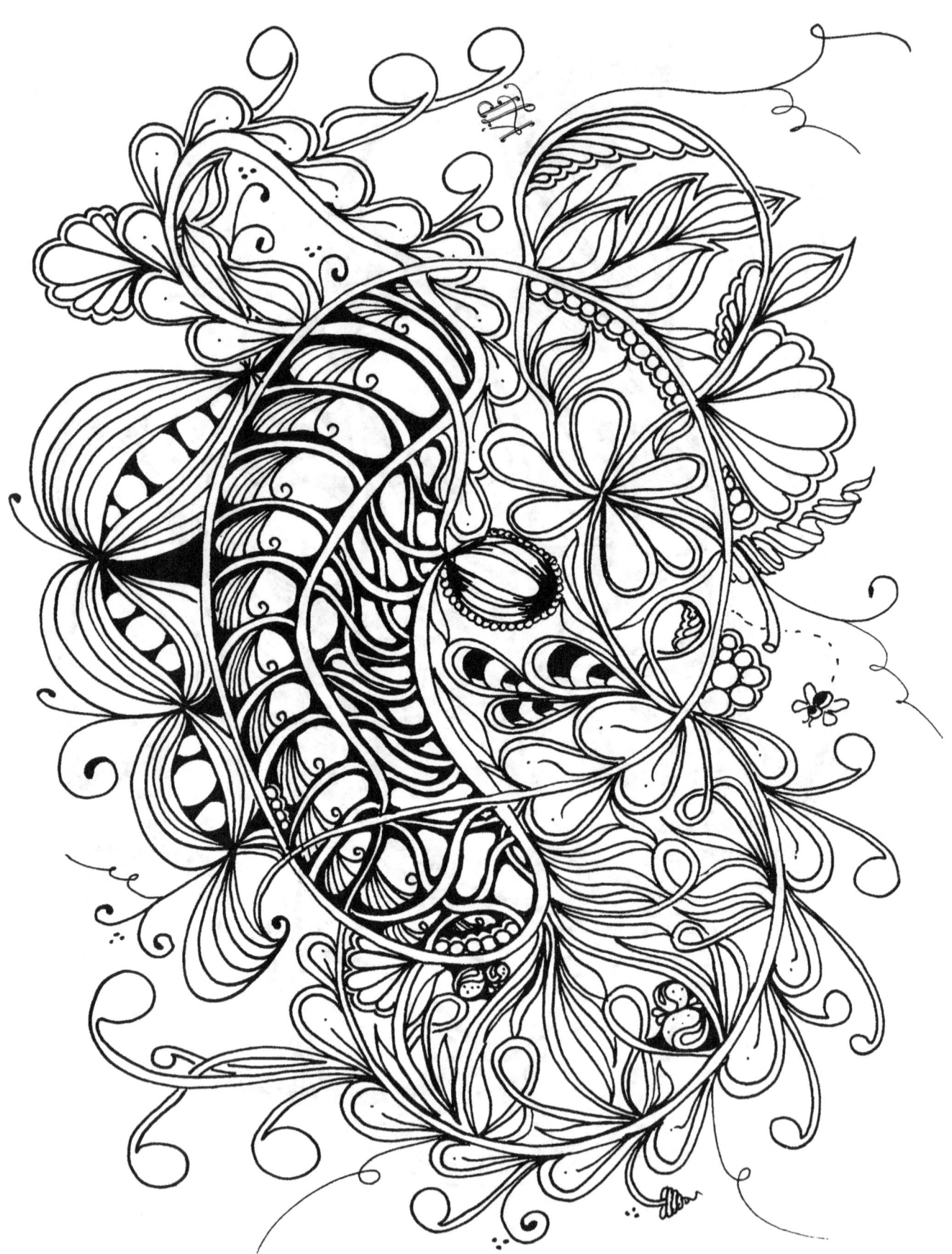

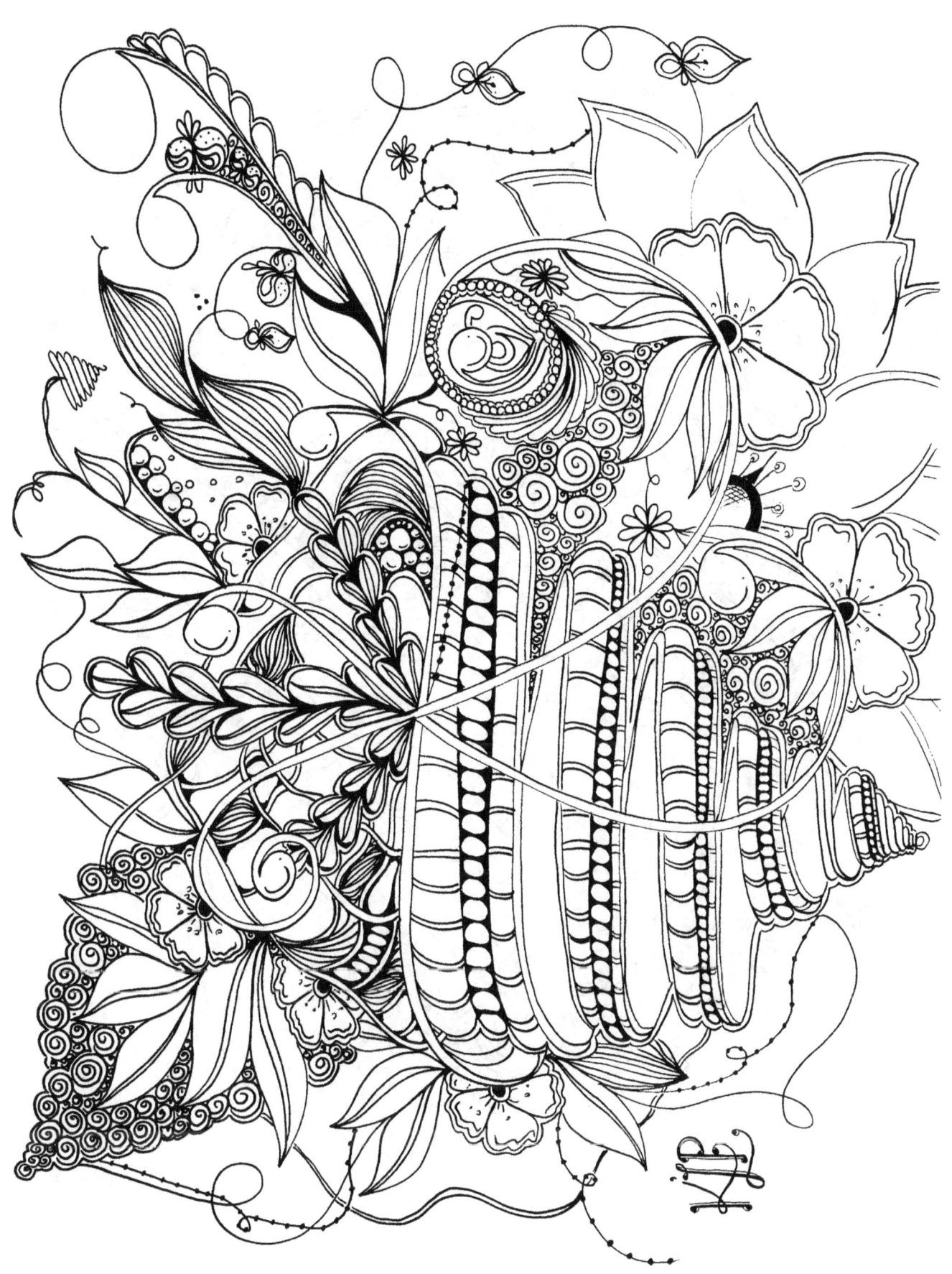

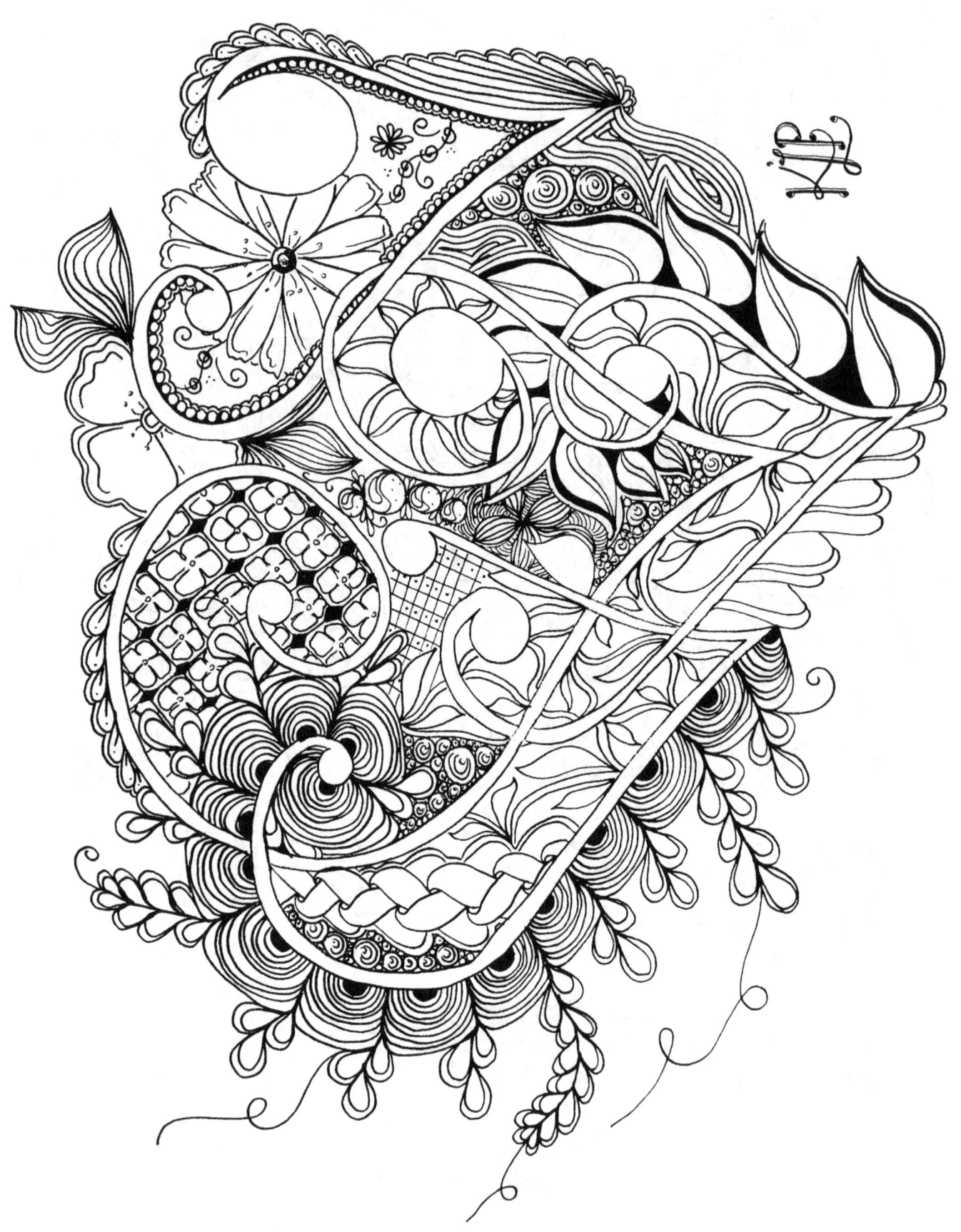

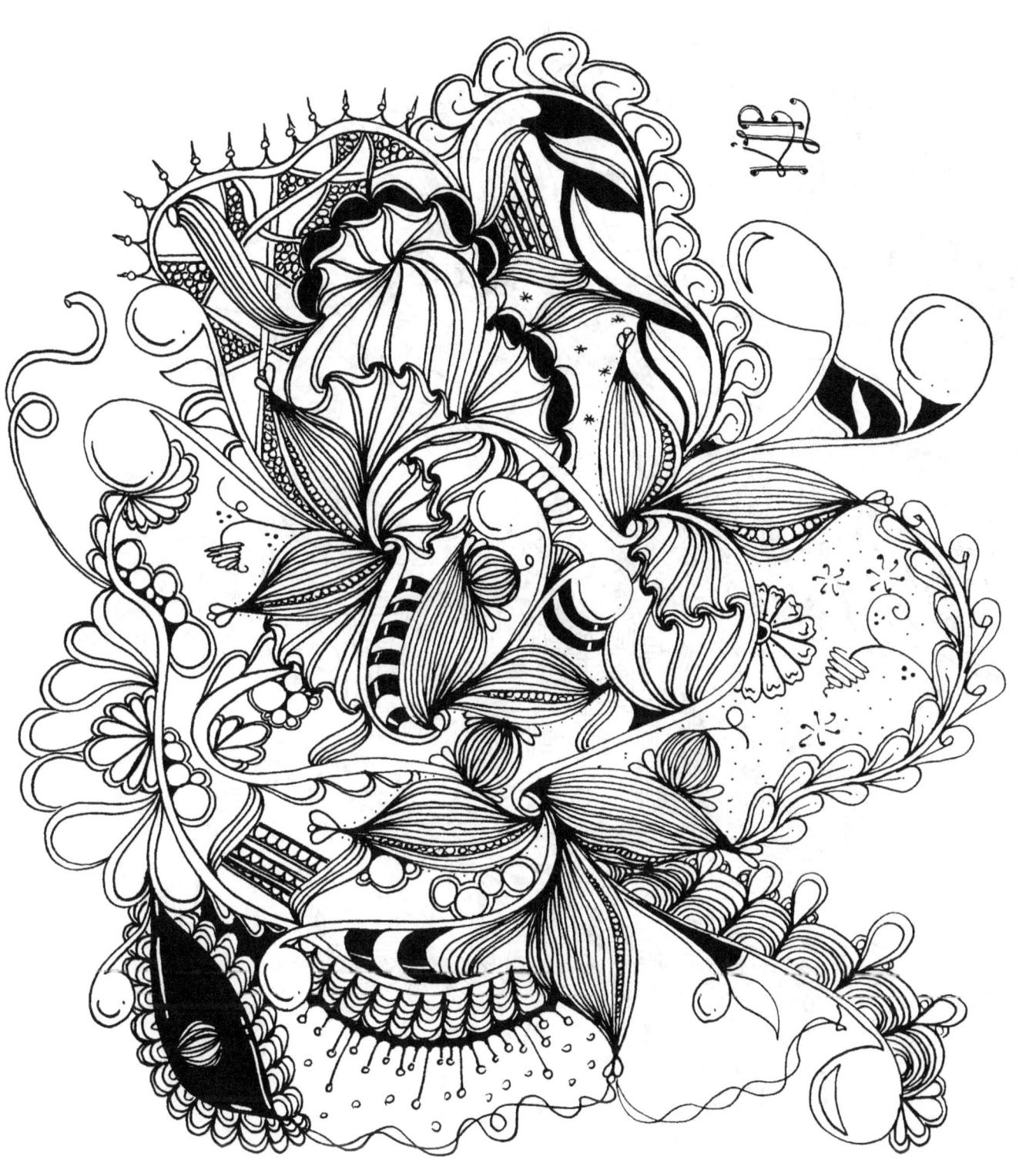

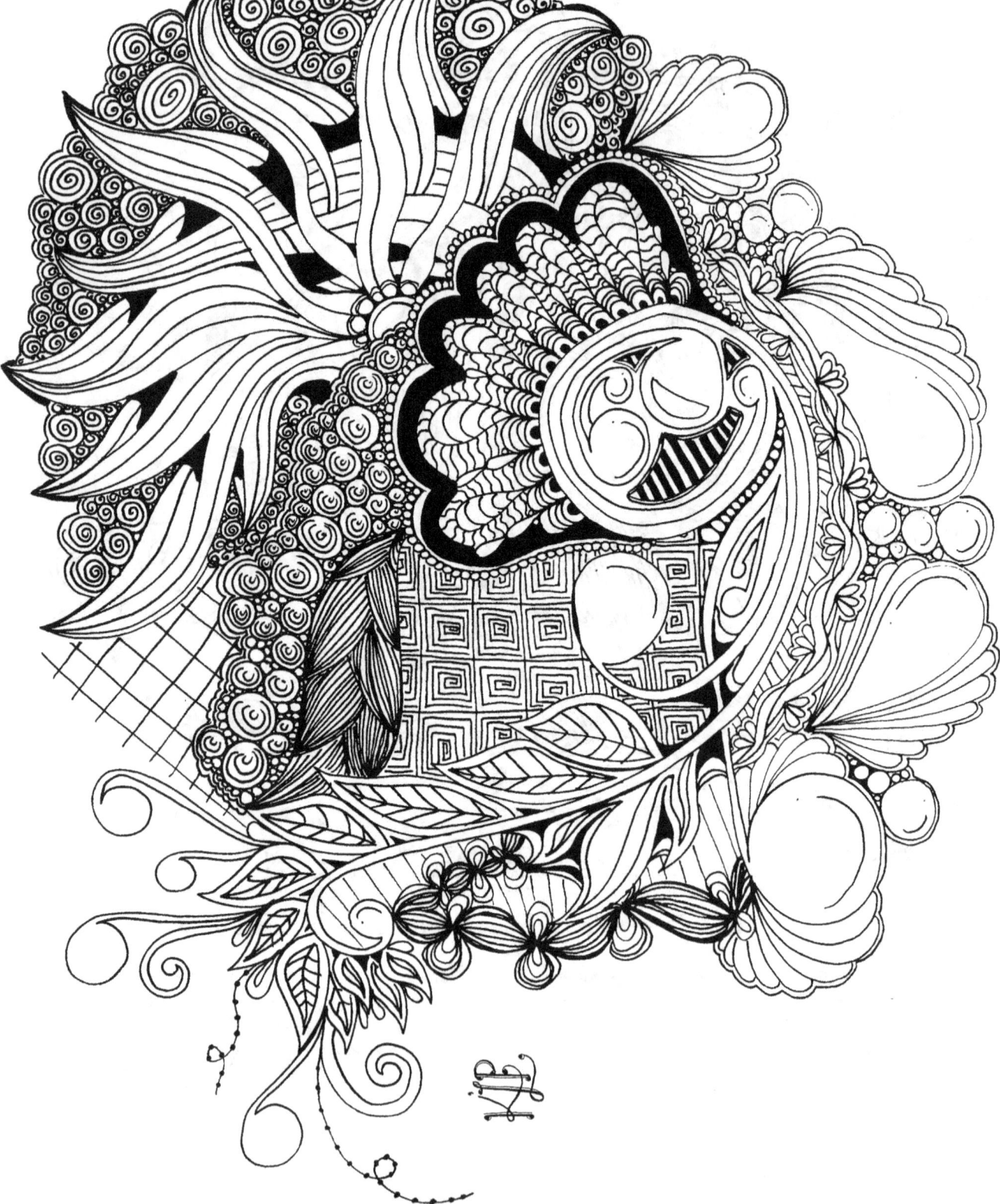

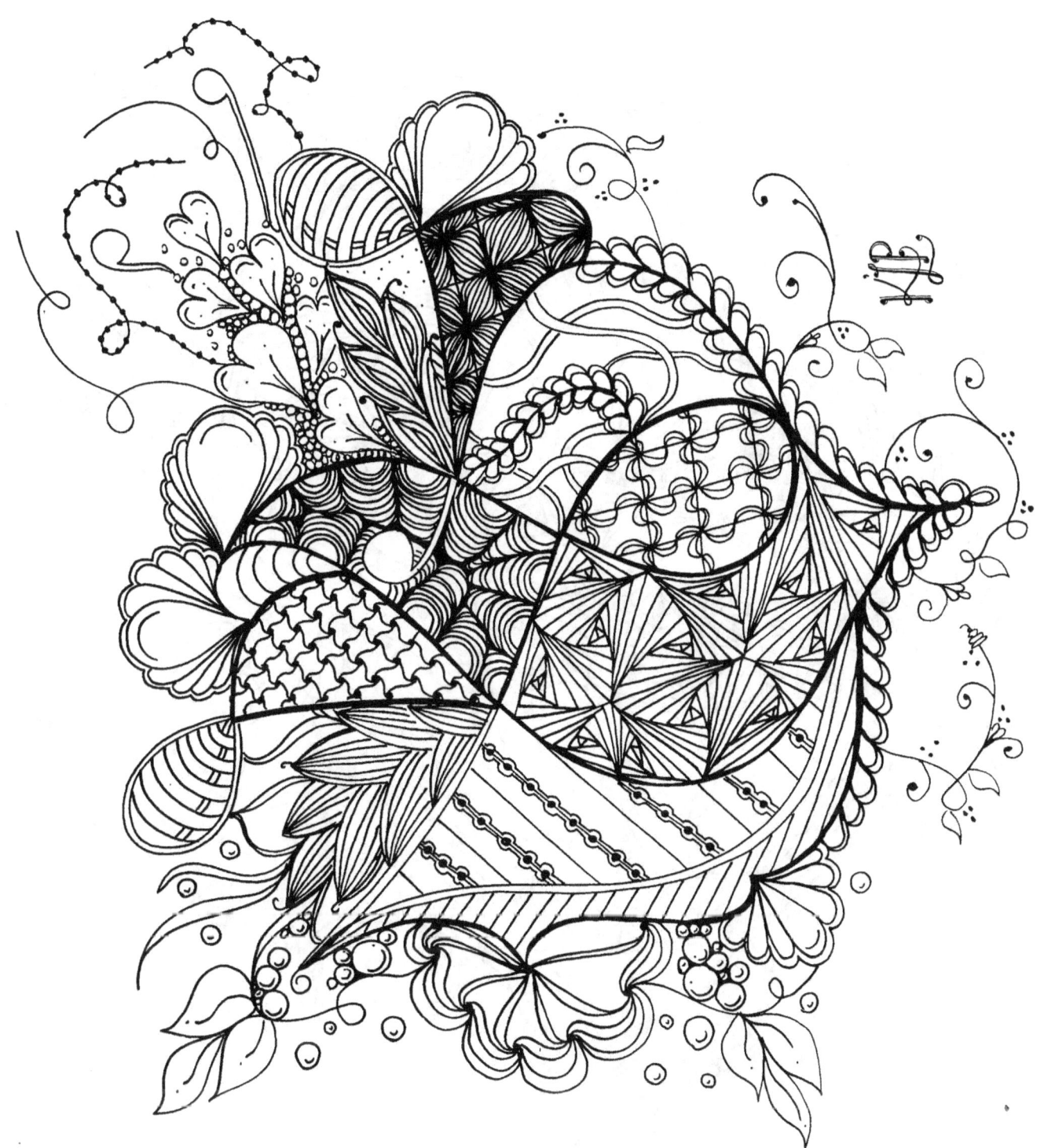

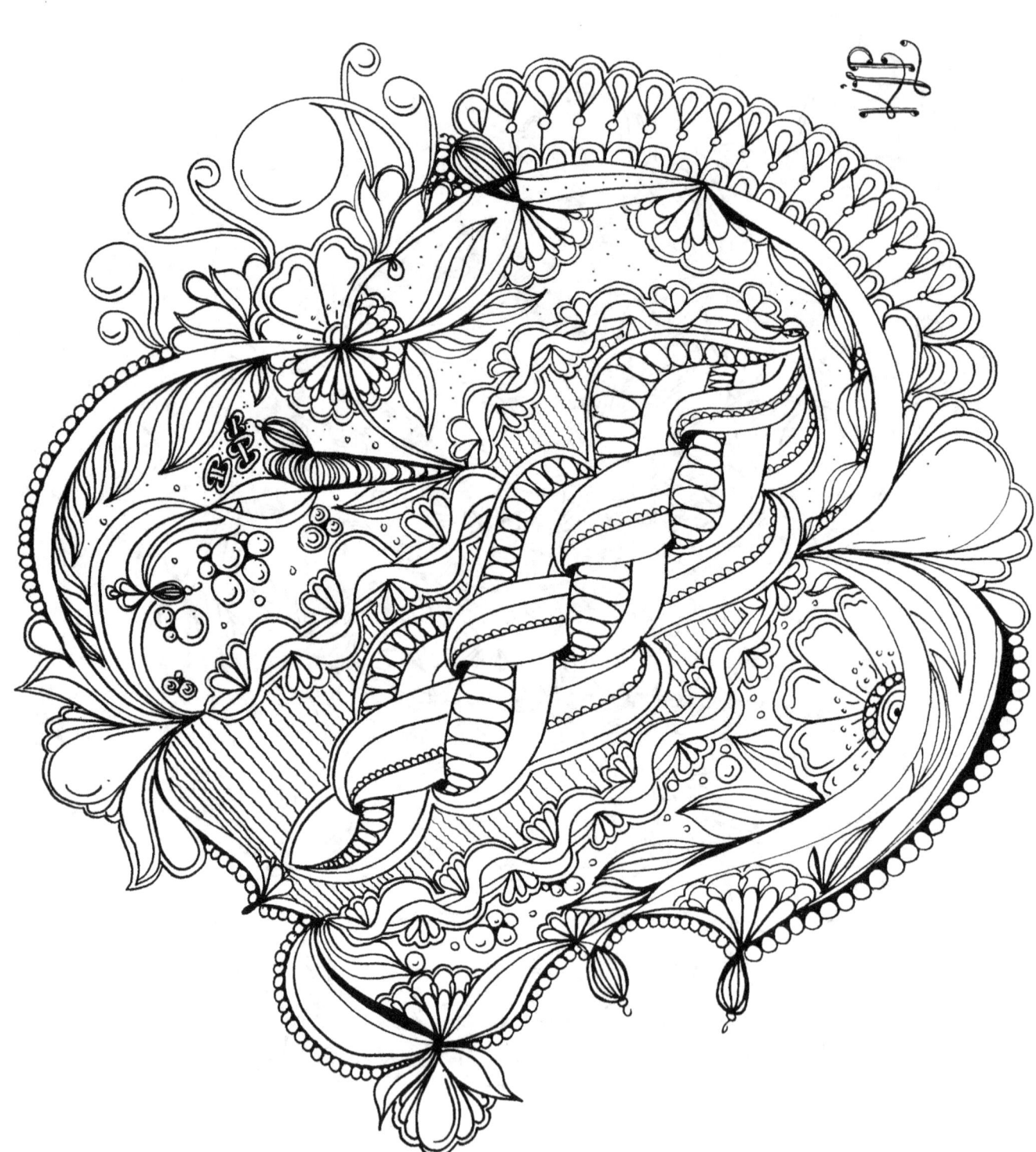

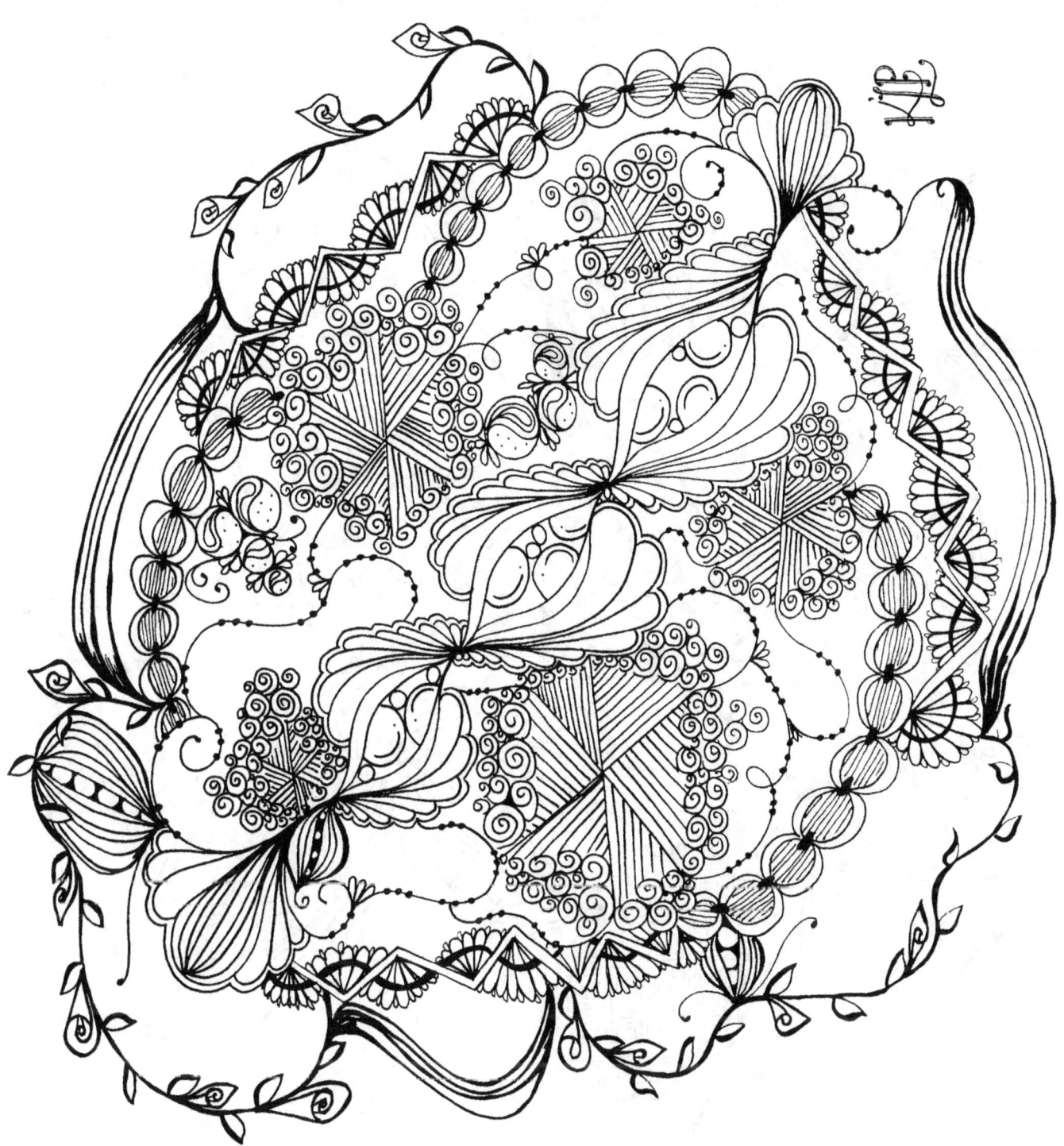

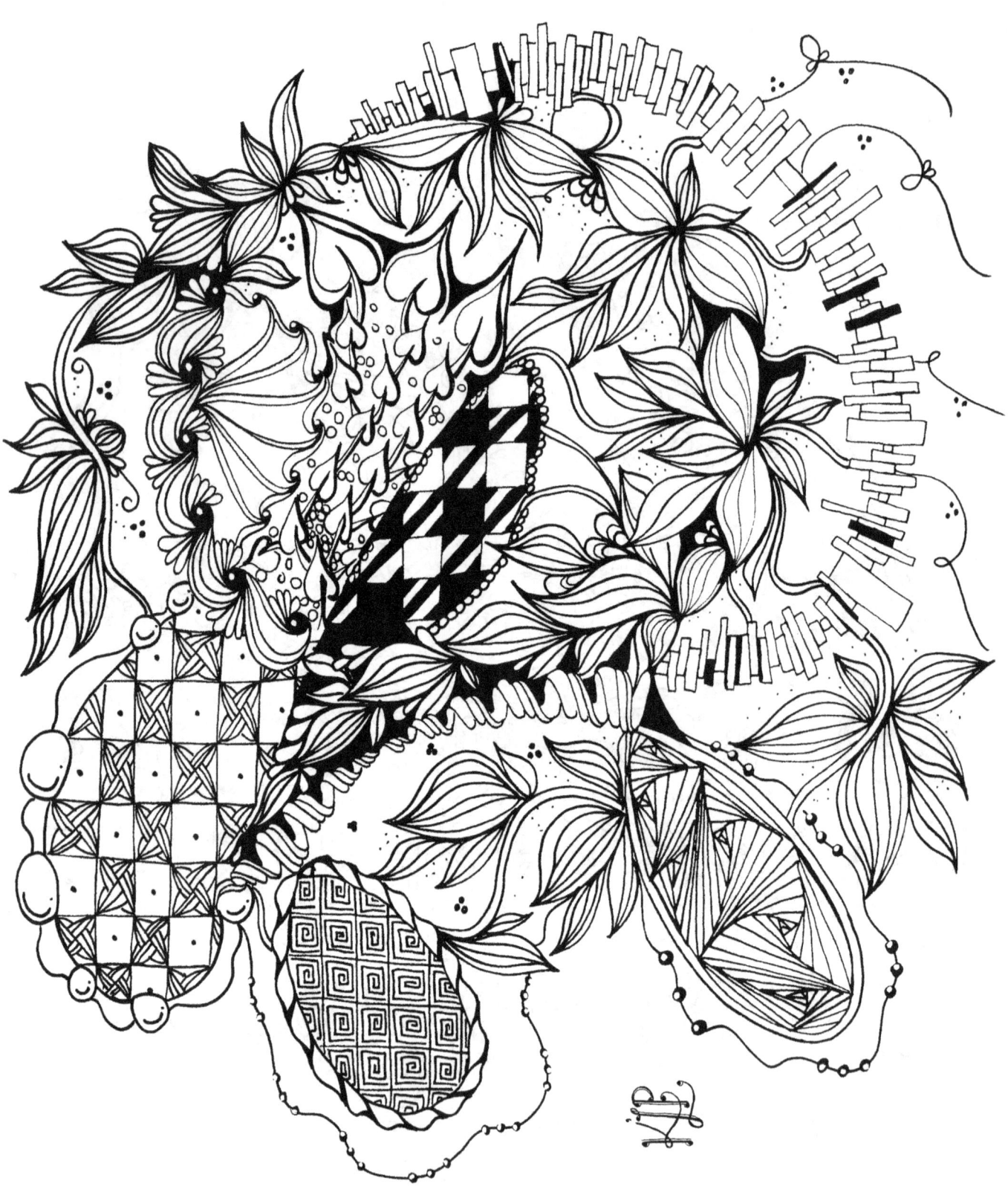

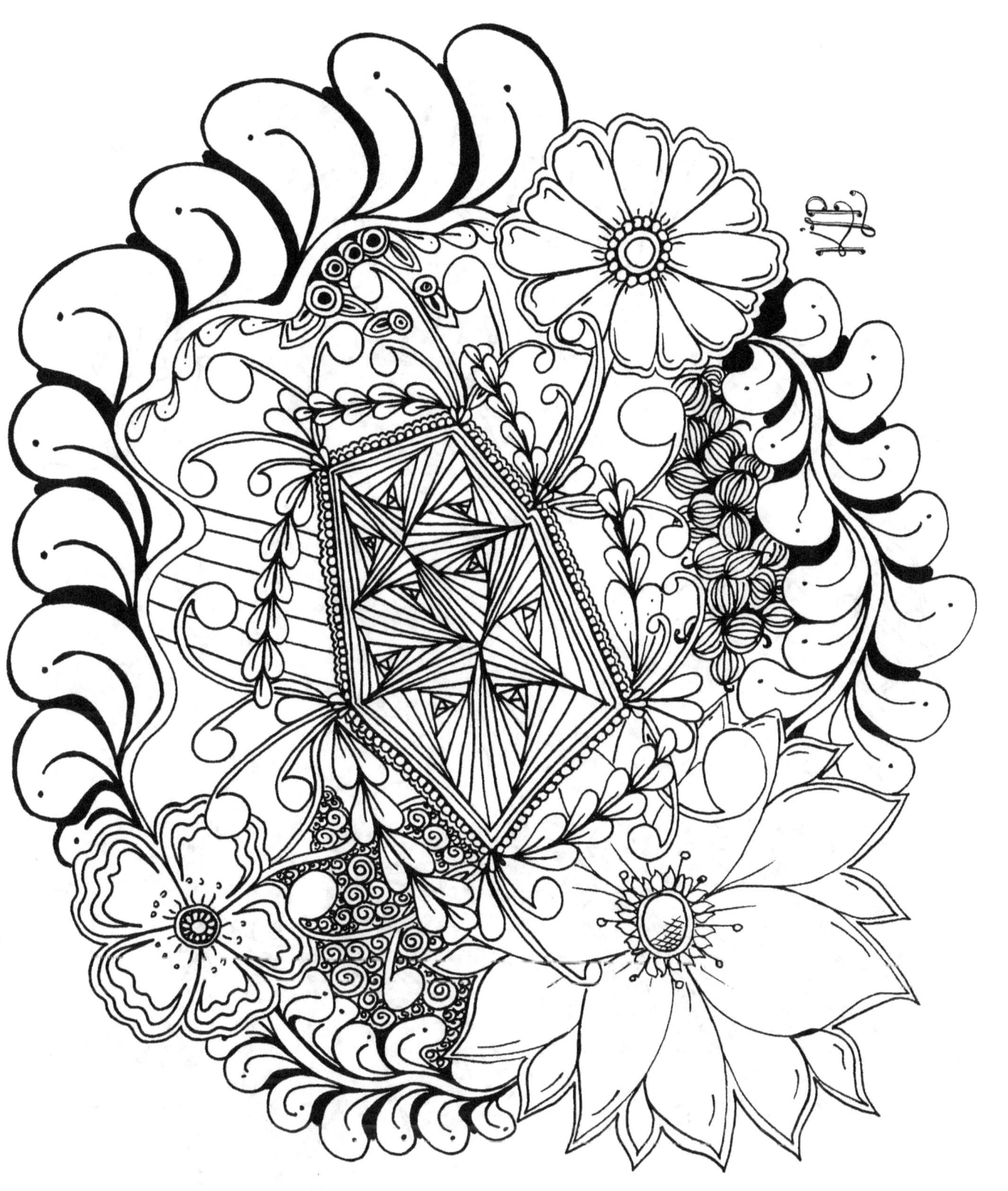

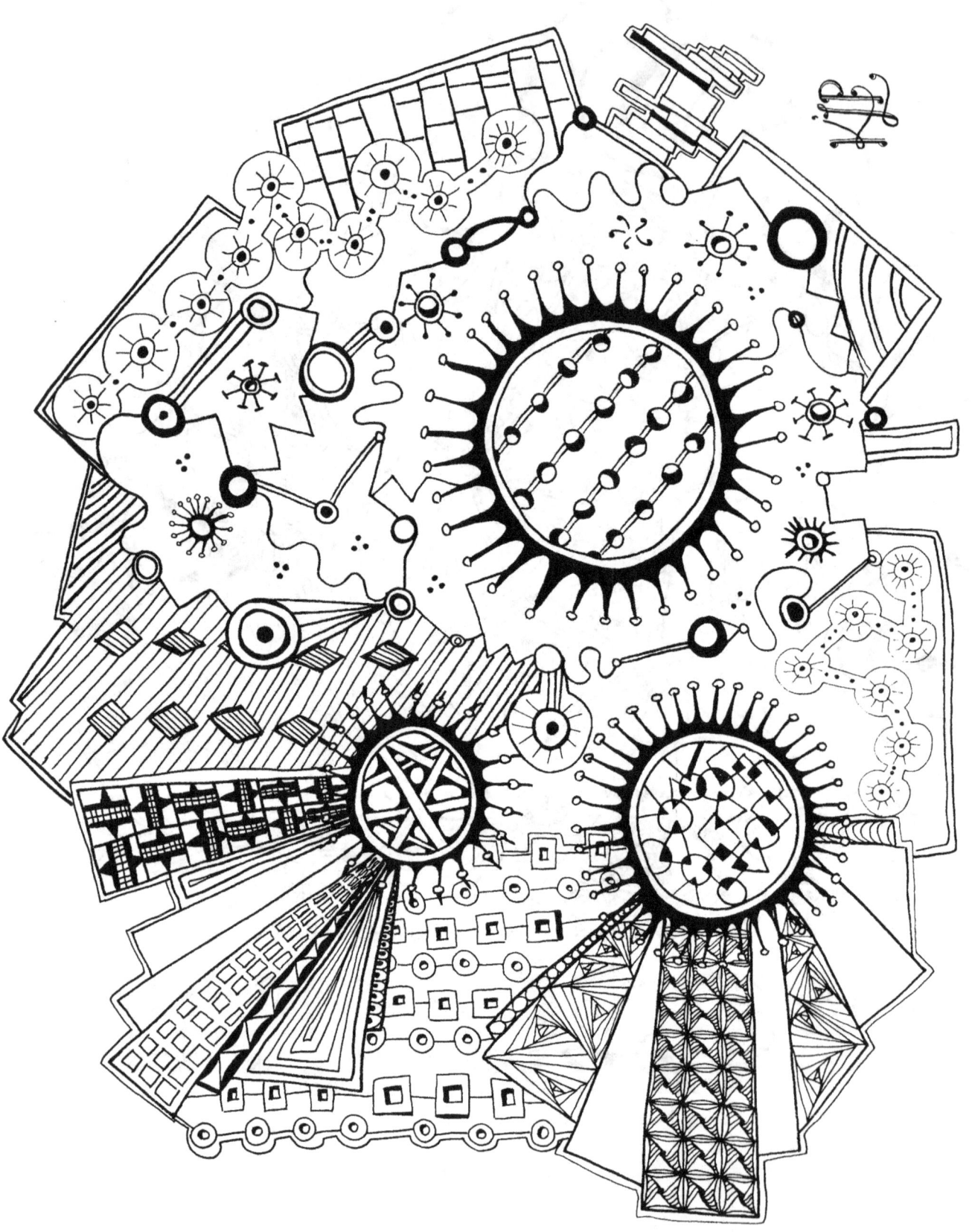

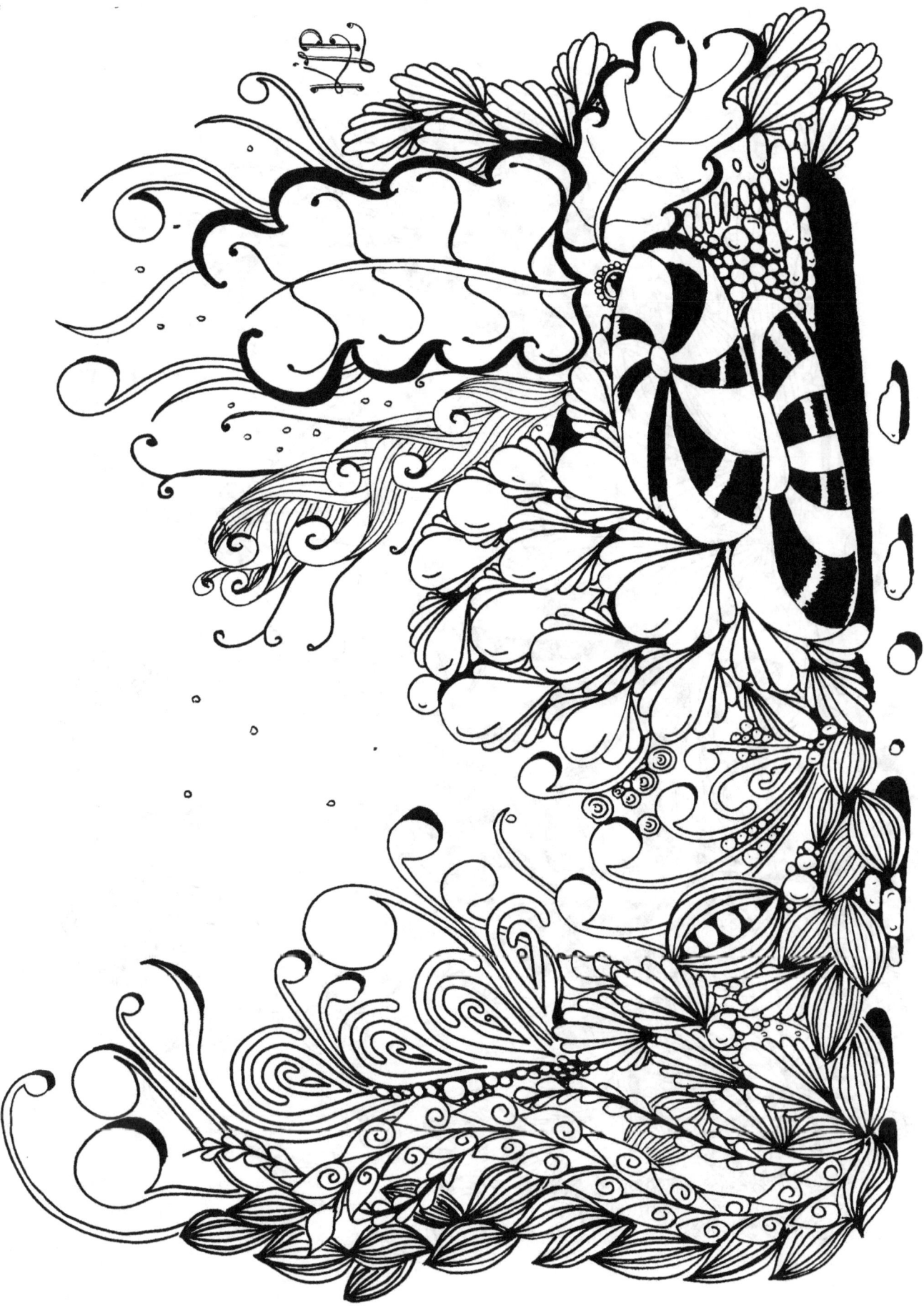

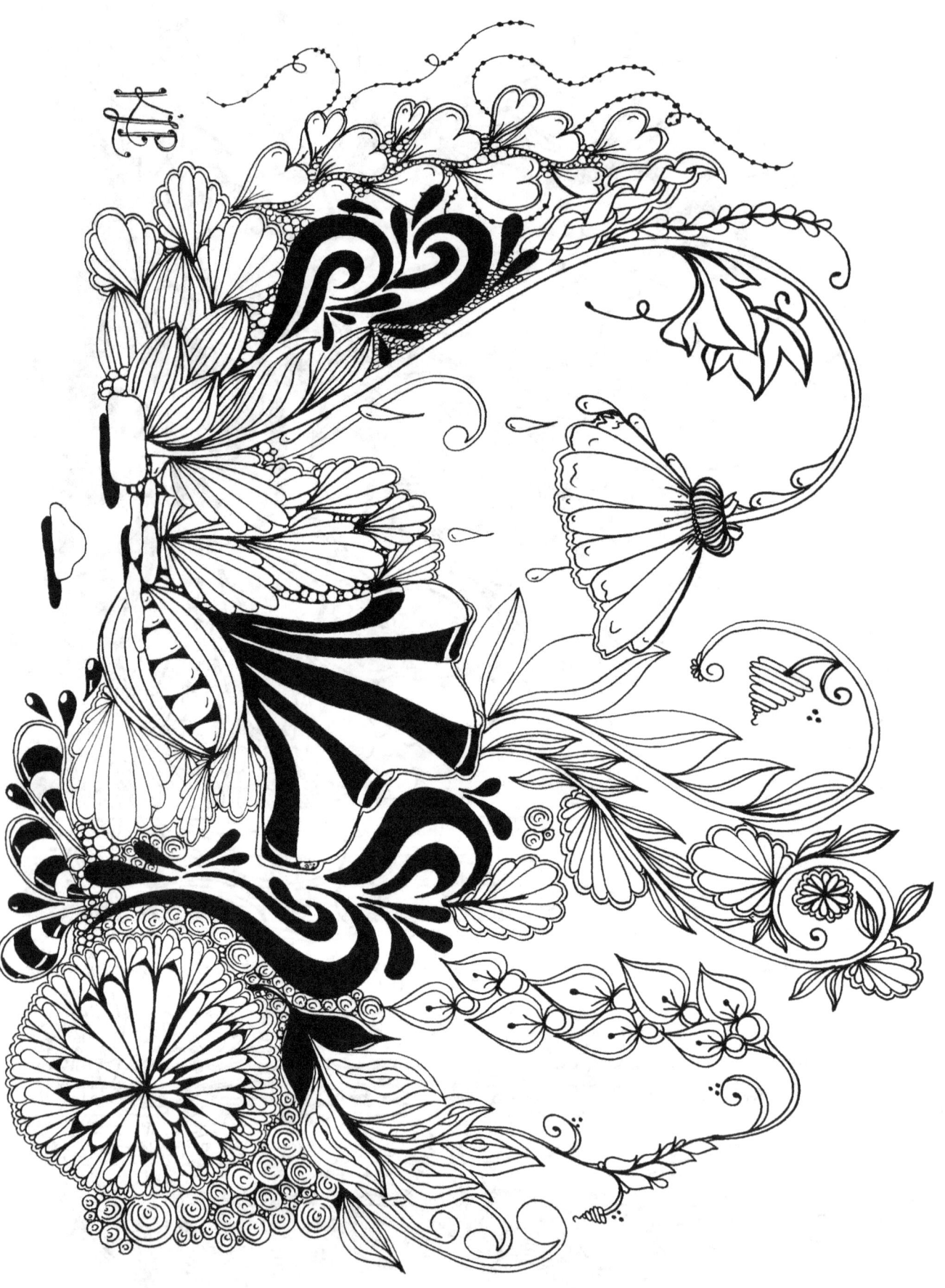

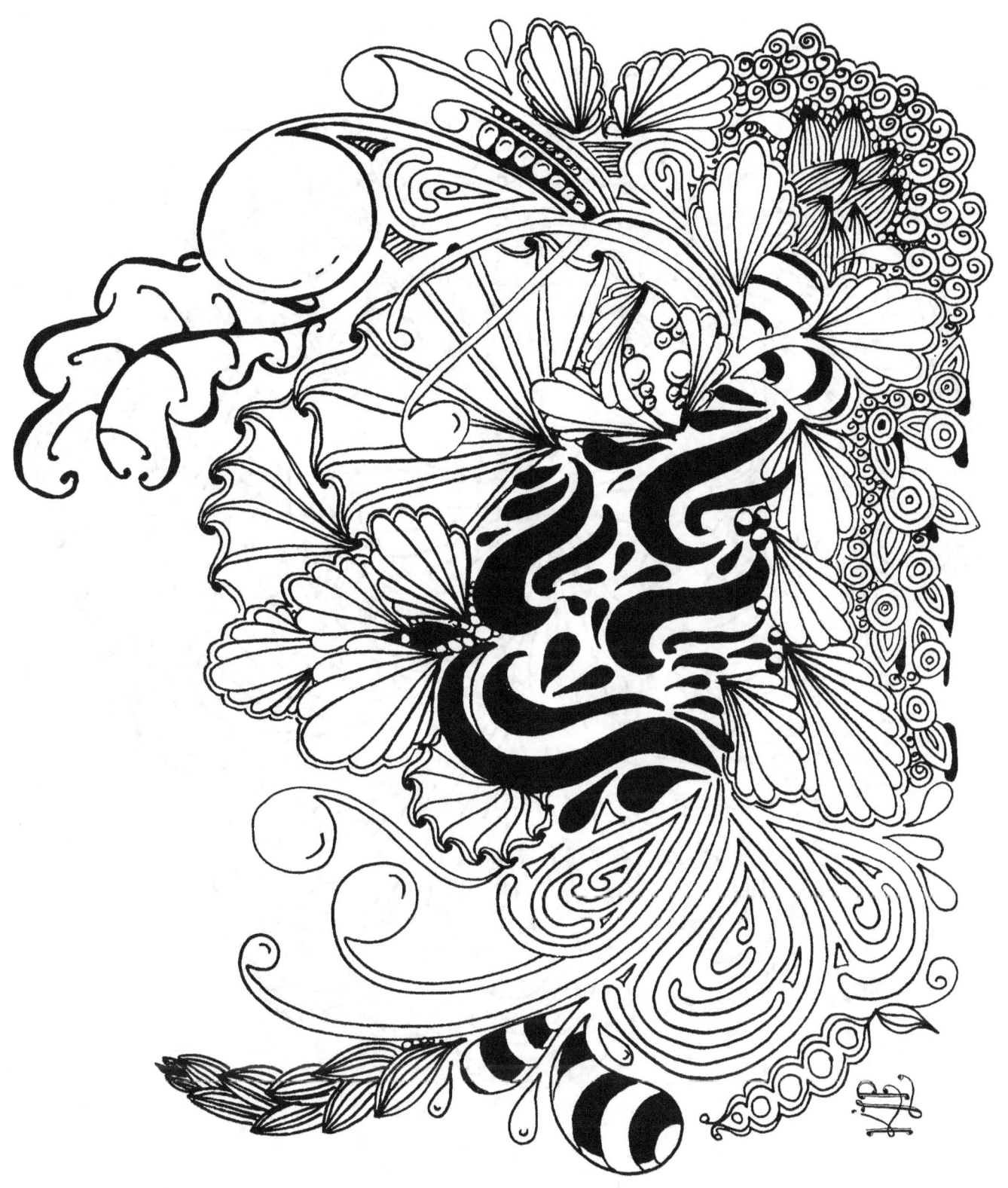

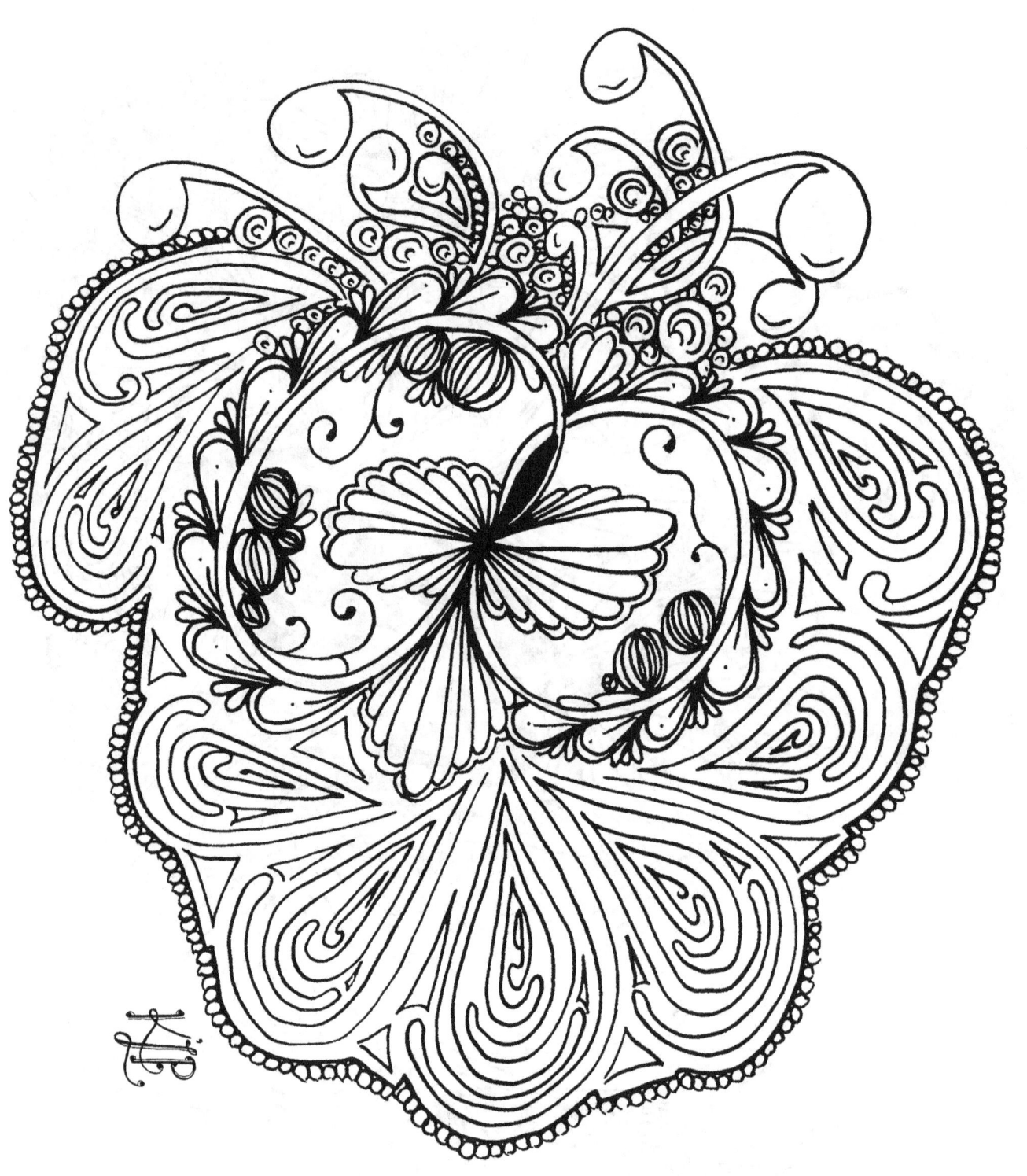

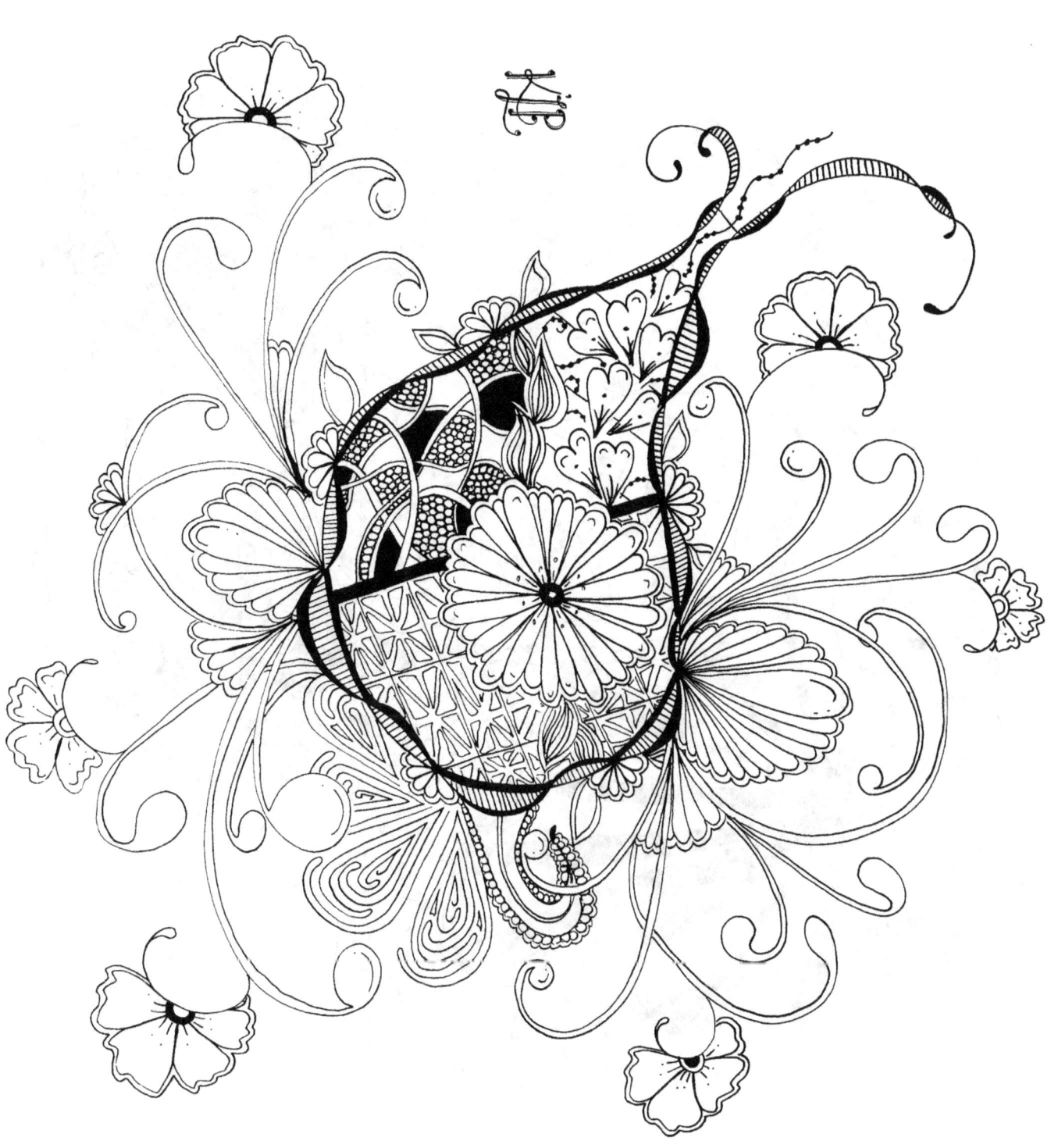

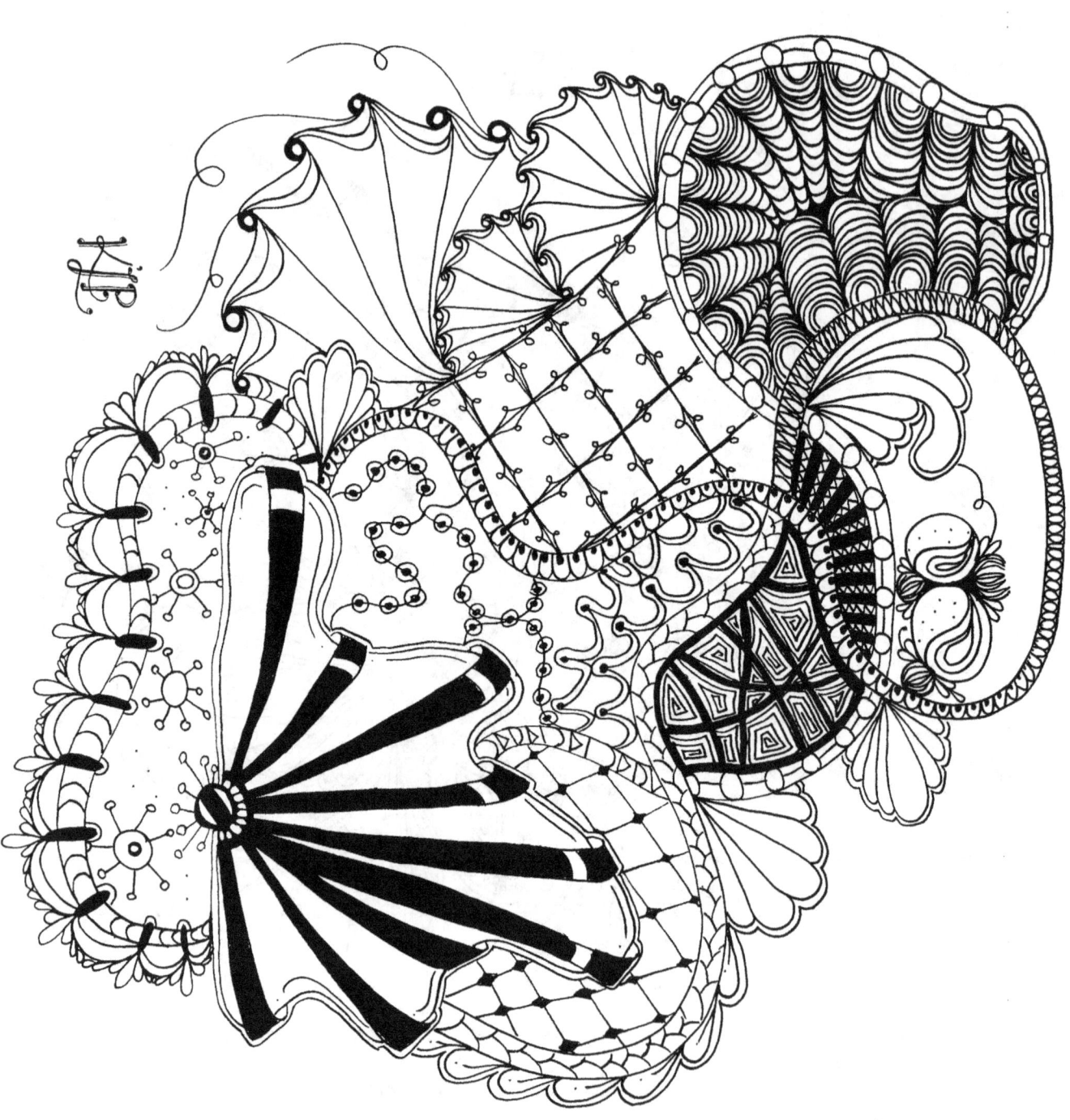

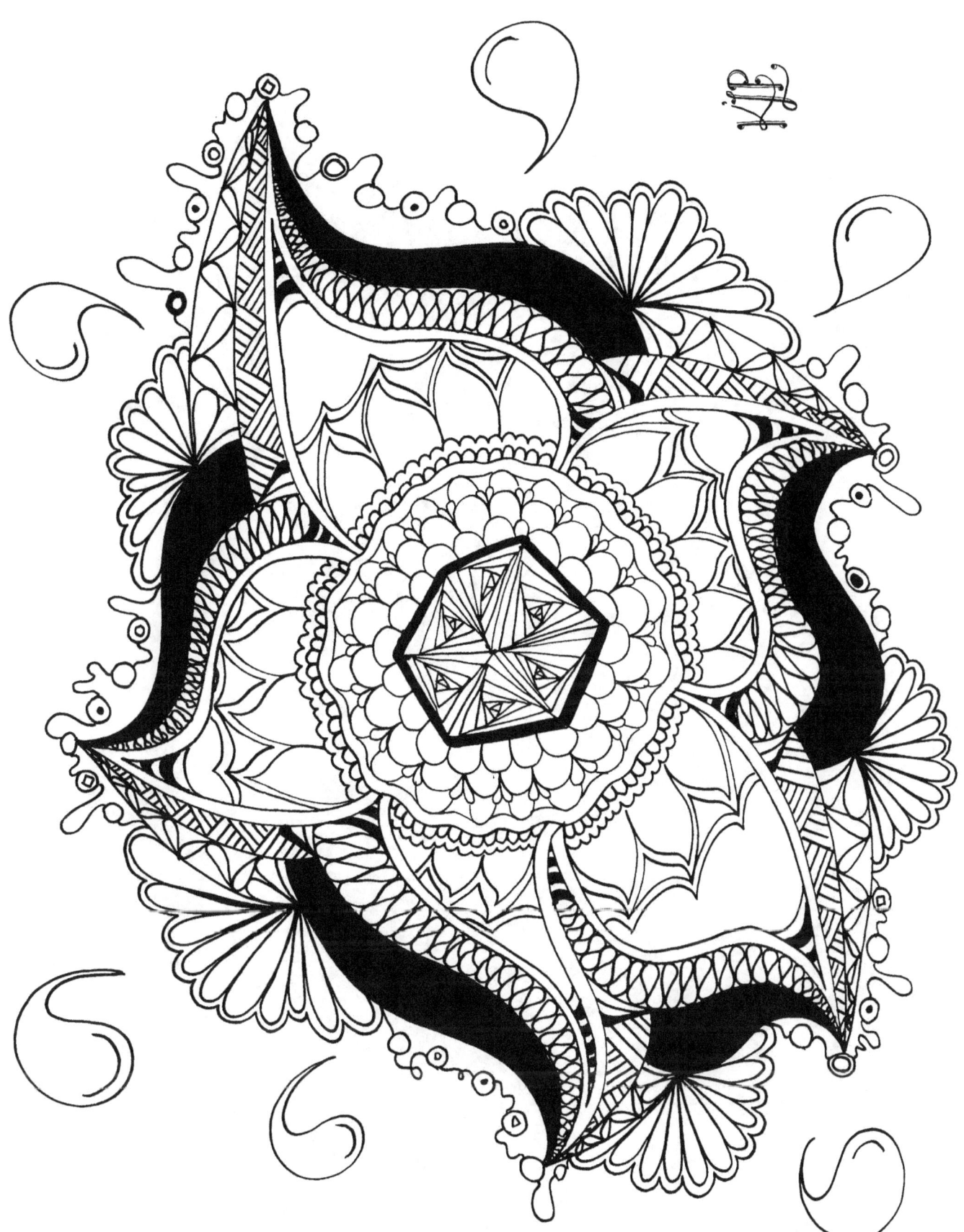